DEVELOPMENTS IN ECONOMETRIC ANALYSES OF PRODUCTIVITY

Studies in Productivity Analysis

Ali Dogramaci, Editor
Cornell University

Titles in the Series:

Adam, Dogramaci; Productivity Analysis at the Organizational Level

Dogramaci, Adam; Aggregate and Industry-Level Productivity Analysis

Dogramaci; Productivity Analysis: A Range of Perspectives

Dogramaci; Developments in Econometric Analyses of Productivity: Measurement and Modelling Issues

Developments in Econometric Analyses of Productivity

Measurement and Modeling Issues

edited by
A. Dogramaci

Kluwer-Nijhoff Publishing
Boston The Hague London

Distributors for North America:
Kluwer.Nijhoff Publishing
Kluwer Boston, Inc.
190 Old Derby Street
Hingham, Massachusetts 02043, U.S.A.

Distributors outside North America:
Kluwer Academic Publishers Group
Distribution Centre
P.O. Box 322
3300AH Dordrecht, The Netherlands

Library of Congress Cataloging in Publication Data
Main entry under title:
Developments in econometric analyses of
productivity: Measurement and Modeling Issues
(Studies in productivity analysis)
Includes bibliographies and indexes.
1. industrial productivity—Mathematical
models—Addresses, essays, lectures. I. Dogramaci,
Ali. II. Series.
HD56.D48 1983 338'.06'0724 82-6456
ISBN O-89838-101-O AACR2

Printed in the United States of America

Contents

Contributing Authors

P.S. Calem, Brown University

T. Cowing, State University of New York at Binghamton

M. Denny, University of Toronto

A. Dogramaci, Cornell University

M. Fuss, University of Toronto

F. M. Gallop, Boston College

W. H. Greene, New York University and National Economic Research Associates

D. Reifschneider, University of Wisconsin, Madison

R. Sato, Brown University

R. Stevenson, University of Wisconsin, Madison

G.T. Woodward, U.S. General Accounting Office

Acknowledgement to Referees

Anonymous refereeing is a process that accompanies every paper that appears in the series Studies in Productivity Analysis. The list below includes the names of reviewers who contributed to the refereeing of at least one paper considered for Studies in Productivity Analysis. To ensure anonymity, the list includes names of a few additional referees who evaluated papers for other volumes of Studies in Productivity Analysis.

We would like to express our deep appreciation for the expert counsel and guidance they have provided.

N. R. Adam	Rutgers The State University of New Jersey
H. Burley	La Trobe University
F. R. Førsund	University of Oslo
W. Gehrig	Karlsruhe University
A. Harrigan	New York University
L. Hjalmarsson	University of Gothenburg
Th. Junius	University of Groningen
J. Kmenta	Michigan State University
K. G. Lofgren	The Swedish University of Agricultural Sciences
C. A. Knox Lovell	University of North Carolina at Chapel Hill
W. Meeusen	State University Centre, Antwerp
R. Ramachandran	Southern Methodist University

P. Schmidt	Michican State University
E. F. Sudit	Rutgers The State University of New Jersey
J. van den Broeck	State University Centre, Antwerp

Development in Econometric Analysis of Productivity

1 ECONOMETRIC APPROACHES TO PRODUCTIVITY MEASUREMENT: A BRIEF OVERVIEW

A. Dogramaci

1.1 Introduction

Productivity measurement and analysis involves observing a series of quantities of outputs produced, inputs used, and their prices. From such data one tries to account for the sources of change in productivity. In order to carry out such analyses, decisions have to be made on how outputs and inputs should be measured and what methods need to be used in order to determine sources of productivity growth—or decline. This volume presents some of the recent econometric modelling and measurement efforts aimed at such questions.

The topics include empirical comparative analysis of labor productivity versus total factor productivity; bias of some total factor productivity estimates due to intermediate goods imported into an economy; some issues related to estimation of production frontiers; measurement of efficiencies of different inputs of production and their rates of change through time

I am indebted to T. Cowing, F. M. Gollop and T. Woodward for their helpful comments and criticisims and to N. R. Adam who handled the refereeing process of this paper.

(estimating variable factor augmentation rates), and related issues on economies of scale and elasticities of substitution.

1.2 Index of Total Factor Productivity

Productivity analyses in this volume are explicitly based on the concept of production functions. A production function denotes the relation between quantities of different varieties of inputs used and the quantities of different varieties of outputs produced at a given period t. Denoting the number of different varieties of inputs and outputs by n and m respectively, let

X_{jt} = quantitiy of jth variety of input used for the production of period t,

Y_{it} = quantity of ith variety of output, produced in period t.

Thus production (frontier) function is a relation that we assume to exist between $X_{1t}, X_{2t}, \ldots, X_{nt}, Y_{1t}, Y_{2t}, \ldots, Y_{mt}$, and it may contain other variables as well. For example the nature of relation between inputs and outputs may change through time. (This is interchangeably called technical change or technological change.) If it is possible to reflect the changing nature of relationship between inputs and outputs by incorporating time (t) into the production function, then t becomes one of the additional variables in the production function.

The roots of total factor productivity go back to the works of Tinbergen (1942), Stigler (1947), Abramovitz (1956), Kendrick (1956), Solow (1957), Denison (1962), Griliches and Jorgenson (1966) and Jorgenson and Griliches (1967). Assuming that the production function conforms to certain differentiability and curvature characteristics, and setting

$Y(t)$ = a consistent index of total output, obtained by aggregating $Y_{1t}, Y_{2t}, \ldots Y_{mt}$ in some manner, and

$X(t)$ = a consistent index of inputs used, obtained by aggregating $X_{1t}, X_{2t}, \ldots X_{nt}$ in some manner,

Berndt (1980) in a brief review, summarized the indexes of total factor productivity $TFP(t)$, for period t, by

$$TFP(t) = \frac{\dot{Y}}{Y(t)} - \frac{\dot{X}}{X(t)} \qquad (1-1)$$

where $\dot{Y}$ and $\dot{X}$ are the time derivatives of $Y(t)$ and $X(t)$ respectively. This index addresses the changes through time. In practice, data are available only for discrete periods of time. Therefore in practice the derivatives in equation (1–1) are replaced by finite differences. If, instead of studying the productivity changes of a system through time, one decides to study the productivity differences of two separate systems at the same point in time, then the t index in the finite differences equation would need to be interpreted as an index to identify the different production systems.[1]

Most of the production functions used in this volume are of the form

$$Y(t) = F(X_{1t}, X_{2t}, \ldots, X_{nt}, t) \tag{1–2}$$

Instead of dealing with production functions, one may choose to deal with (factor minimal) cost functions C, of the following form:

$$\left.\begin{array}{l}\text{minimum total cost of producing}\\ \text{output } Y(t) \text{ under prices } P_{1t},\\ P_{2t}, \ldots\ P_{nt} \text{ for the } n \text{ inputs}\end{array}\right\} = C[Y(t), P_{1t}, P_{2t}, \ldots P_{nt}, t] \tag{1–3}$$

Equation (1–2) may be called a primal model, and equation (1–3) can be denoted as the dual model. Some of the major research on the duality between production and cost functions include works of Shephard (1953, 1970), Uzawa (1964), Diewert (1971), and papers in Fuss and McFadden (1978). Throughout this volume it will be assumed that F and C satisfy certain differentiability and curvature characteristics. In addition to expressing an index of total factor productivity as given in equation (1–1), it is also possible to use as a measure, the partial derivative of F with respect to time t, holding all input quantities fixed. Such an index of technical change, being based on the primal model (1–2), is called the primal rate of total factor productivity. Suppose we denote it by τ. Then,

$$\tau = \partial \ln F/\partial r. \tag{1–4}$$

Using duality one can construct another index related to total factor productivity. For a given set of input prices and output quantity, the partial derivative of the (factor minimal) cost function C with respect to t also indicates technical change. If we denote it by λ, then:

$$\lambda = -\,\partial \ln C/\partial t \tag{1–5}$$

λ is called the rate of cost dimunition. In this volume, chapters five and six use this dual index, and chapters two, three and seven use primal measures of total factor productivity. Ohta (1974) showed that τ is related to λ as follows:

$$\tau = \lambda/\varepsilon \tag{1–6}$$

where

$$\varepsilon = \partial \ln C / \partial \ln Y \qquad (1\text{–}7)$$

The reciprocal of ε is an index of returns to scale. When constant returns to scale is imposed $\varepsilon = 1$ and thus $\tau = \lambda$.

1.3. Total Factor Productivity versus Labor Productivity

In spite of econometricians' emphasis on total factor productivity, a partial measure of productivity, namely that of labor, has remained as the single most widely discussed index in the mass media. Most of the mass-circulation public documents limit their discussions on productivity to output per man-hour; and it may not be farfetched to assume that many executives in public as well as private organizations feel more comfortable to think in labor productivity terms, rather than in total factor productivity measures. Thus it becomes of interest to observe the interrelation versus differences between labor productivity and total factor productivity, in a comparative study of a major industrial country. The next chapter of this volume does precisely that.

In a recent study, Denny, Fuss and May (1981) compared the variation in total factor productivity growth among different regions of Canada. In chapter 2, Denny and Fuss extend their analysis to levels of labor productivity. Covering a time span from 1961 to mid-1970s they compare labor versus total factor productivities of major regions of Canada. They find that while total factor productivity differences generally are in the same direction with labor productivity, in terms of magnitude, they are substantially smaller.

In this chapter Denny and Fuss also show,

1. what portion of the variations in labor productivity are due to changes in ratios of capital to labor, and materials to labor; and
2. what portion of the variations in labor productivity are due to growth in total factor productivity.

They find that the variations of factor intensities between different regions, have a stronger effect on labor productivity than do the variations of total factor productivity.

1.4. Influence of Imported Intermediate Inputs on Productivity Measures

The third chapter of the volume addresses the following question: Can total factor productivity measures for the aggregate economy be affected by the dependence of an economy on imported material? In this chapter Gollop analyses the alternatives of basing the aggregate studies on measures of value added, versus on "deliveries to final demand." The latter approach takes into account both the intersectoral as well as the international aspects about transactions of intermediate materials.

In previous research Gollop (1979), and Gollop and Roberts (1981b) had shown the importance of accounting for intermediate goods. In the present study, Gollop extends this line of research. He shows that existence of imported intermediate goods may cause total factor productivity studies based on value added measures to yield upward bias in their productivity growth estimates. He illustrates this point in Table 3.2 of chapter 3, by comparing the average productivity growths of Canada, France, Germany, Italy, Japan, Netherlands, United Kingdom, and United States for the years 1957–1973. Using a deliveries-to-final-demand approach, rather than the traditional value-added approach, reduces the average productivity growth of Netherlands from 2.33% to 1.59%. On the other hand for United States, which used substantially less imported intermediate goods, the values are 1.23% versus 1.17% respectively.

1.5. Frontier Functions

While total factor productivity analyses study shifts in the average production function, it is also of interest to estimate a maximum production possibility frontier, and observe to what extent firms fall below this frontier. Alternately, one can make use of duality theory. [See Førsund and Jansen (1977), Schmidt and Lovell (1979) and Greene (1980) for estimation of cost frontiers.] In this case one measures how much above the cost frontier do the firms lie.

The research related to frontier functions includes the works of Farrell (1957); Aigner and Chu (1968); Timmer (1971); Afriat (1972); Johansen (1972); Førsund and Hjalmarsson (1974, 1979); Schmidt (1976); Aigner, Lovell, and Schmidt (1977); Meeusen and van den Broeck (1977a, 1977b); the studies collected in Aigner and Schmidt (1980); and Kopp (1981).

In chapter 4, Cowing, Reifschneider, and Stevenson follow this line of study, using a translog cost frontier with alternative specifications of the error term indicating the inefficiencies of the firms. Different distributions of the error term are tested using two separate estimation methods for the cost frontier, in order to find whether a sophisticated and computationaly difficult approach (a maximum likelihood approach) provides significantly different results than standard ordinary least squares (OLS). The analysis is carried out on data for electric utilities and the convenience of OLS is noted in the following sense. When the correlation between

1. the disturbance term of the cost function, and
2. the disturbance terms of the partial derivatives of the cost equation with respect to input prices

are negligible, if one is only interested in estimating the shape of the frontier without individually estimating how different firms are efficient (or inefficient), then OLS can get certain results with considerable ease.

1.6. Productivity of Inputs Used, Elasticity of Substitution, and Economies of Scale

Technological progress can be thought of as the upward shifting of the production function. Increasing returns to scale, on the other hand, deals with a given (nonshifting) production function, of such a shape that if we increase the quantity of inputs used by a certain proportion h, the increase in output will be more than h-fold. The question is, if in the given time series the inputs and outputs tend to increase (on the average) through time, then how can we disentangle the growth due to scale effect from growth due to technical progress? The importance of the question is reflected in the discussions between Stigler (1961) and Solow (1961). Recent developments for separately accounting for scale effect versus technical progress include the works of Ohta (1974), Christensen and Greene (1976), Berndt and Khaled (1979), Førsund and Hjalmarsson (1979), Gollop and Roberts (1981a), Stevenson (1980), and Nadiri and Schankerman (1981), and Caves, Christensen and Swanson (1981).

An additional difficulty arises from trying to simultaneously estimate (1) elasticity of substitution between inputs, and (2) amounts of biased technical change. The issues can be described by considering $Y(t)$ (the output in period t) as a function of capital $K(t)$, and labor $L(t)$, augmented by efficiency factors $A(t)$, and $B(t)$ as follows.

$$Y(t) = F[A(t)K(t),\ B(t)L(t)] \tag{1–8}$$

The factor augmentation coefficients $A(t)$ and $B(t)$ are indicators of the productivities in period t, of capital and labor respectively. For example, $B(t) < B(t')$ would imply that a unit of labor used in period t' would produce more output than that in period t, if the quality and quantity of capital available in both periods was the same.

To describe the problem, we shall use Sato's (1970) argumentation. Using his notation we set

$$K' = A(t)K(t)$$
$$L' = B(t)L(t)$$

$$\dot{A}/A = \frac{dA(t)/dt}{A(t)}$$

$$\dot{B}/B = \frac{dB(t)/dt}{B(t)}$$
$$x = L(t)/K(t)$$
$$y = Y(t)/K(t)$$
$$z = Y(t)/L(t)$$

$\sigma =$ elasticity of substitution between capital and labor: a measure of the ease of substitutability between capital and labor, holding $Y(\cdot)$ constant.

$$\sigma = \frac{\dfrac{d(K'/L')}{K'/L'}}{\dfrac{d\left(\dfrac{\partial F/\partial L'}{\partial F/\partial K'}\right)}{\dfrac{\partial F/\partial L'}{\partial F/\partial K'}}} \tag{1-9}$$

where $\dot{A}/A$ is the rate of growth of efficiency of capital, also called factor augmentation rate for capital or rate of technical progress for capital, and $\dot{B}/B$ is the rate of growth of efficiency of labor, also called factor augmentation rate for labor or rate of technical progress for labor. (While the above equations treat the dynamics of change as a continuous process, in practice we are confined to data observed at discrete points in time, such as annual or quarterly or monthly data. Thus in practice one uses approximations such as $\Delta A(t)/A(t)$ instead of $\dot{A}/A$, and $\Delta B(t)$ instead of $\dot{B}/B$.)

Assuming competitive markets that pay factors of production their marginal products, wage rate is denoted by w and return on capital by r. Sato (1970) shows that if F in equation (1–8) is linear, homogenous of degree one, and continuously differentiable with respect to all the variables up to a desired level then, without specifying the functional form of F, one can still relate the rates of growth of efficiency of capital and labor to the elasticity of substitution as follows, provided that $\sigma \neq 1$.

$$\dot{A}/A = \frac{\sigma(\dot{r}/r) - \dot{y}/y}{\sigma - 1} \tag{1–10}$$

$$\dot{B}/B = \frac{\sigma(\dot{w}/w) - \dot{z}/z}{\sigma - 1} \tag{1–11}$$

Thus one has three unknowns $\dot{A}/A$, $\dot{B}/B$, and σ, but only two equations. This is called the "Diamond-McFadden nonidentification problem" because, for a time series, without choosing a specific functional form for F or assuming that either elasticity of substitution or factor augmentation rate is constant through time, one cannot estimate all simultaneously for a time series (Diamond and McFadden, 1965.)

The approach given in Sato (1970) is to study the given time series data with different production function, including constant elasticity of substitution (CES) production functions, as well as constant elasticity of derived demand (CEDD) production functions. Each production function is investigated for different choices of σ. For CES the choices are merely different constants. For CEDD, the choices are different functions of σ. In each such alternative, using the values of σ, the values of $\dot{A}/A$ and $\dot{B}/B$ are computed for every period t. Next, the average values of $\dot{A}/A$ and $\dot{B}/B$ over the entire number of periods are computed. Based on these average values a new set of series are generated for $A(t)$ and $B(t)$ and used to estimate the regression equation for the production function.

Another approach to the whole problem (as discussed by Diamond, McFadden and Rodriguez, 1978) is to assume that

$$\dot{A}/A = \sum_{i=1}^{n} a_i(t) \cdot \theta_i \qquad \text{and} \qquad \dot{B}/B = \sum_{i=1}^{n} b_i(t) \cdot \theta_i$$

The values of $a_i(t)$ and $b_i(t)$ are to be chosen by the researcher and the values of θ_i then can be empirically determined making use of a theorem by Diamond, McFadden, and Rodriguez (1978, pp. 144–145).

In the last three chapters of the volume, several new developments are presented in regard to the estimation of returns to scale, elasticities of substitution, and rates of growth of efficiencies of inputs. In chapter 5 Woodward presents a new method, which is a kind of inversion of Sato's (1970) method. He first fits to the available time series a long-run translog cost function with constant rates of technical change, in order to obtain the estimates of elasticities of substitution (or regression parameters related to the elasticities of substitution). These results are used to generate series of labor-augmenting and capital-augmenting technical change, on a variable rate basis. The structure of the cost function and technical change chosen by Woodward does not distinguish between economies of scale and technical change, since this is not the main focus of his research work.

In chapter 6, Greene begins his analysis by specifying a translog cost function which he later uses to analyze data consisting of time series of cross sections. Naturally, availability of cross section data through time, provides a relief from the difficulties of simultaneous estimation we would have with one set of time series. He develops some general results for decomposing changes in costs and factor demands over time into scale, substitutions, and technological change effects. The paper also includes an estimation methodology that can be classified as in between the method of Berndt and Khaled (1979) and Stevenson (1980). Greene extends the methodology for decomposing rates of change in factor demands and for estimation of differential technological effect over several periods.

In chapter 7 several new developments are presented by Sato and Calem. These developments include generalization of Sato's (1970) earlier method to more than two input factors and its extention for separate estimation of technical progress and scale effect; estimation of technical progress independently of the form of the production function; and a method for estimating productivity growth in a dynamic context with varying forms of production function. The development in chapter 7 also differs from the previous two chapters in the sense that the work is carried out on the primal production function, without resorting to cost functions and duality. These developments find their roots in Sato's pioneering work in the application of Lie group theory to economics (Sato, 1980 and 1981).

1.7. Final Remarks

There are alternative methods for studying productivity. Such alternatives do not necessarily have to contradict each other. For example compare equation (1.8) with (1.2). Equation (1.8) considers only two inputs (capital, K and labor, L) but assumes that for example, one unit of capital in period t+1 is equivalent to R units of capital of period t (where R is a positive number:

R = A(t+1)/A(t)). Now, let us interpret equation (1.2) as follows: n is a large number such that R is equal to 1.0 for any of the input categories. Modelling a production system by equation (1.8) will enable us to study the variations in factor shares (between K and L) as well as the effects of the factor augmentation rates. On the other hand modelling the same production by equation (1.2) will only focus on the variations of factor shares. Does this mean (1.2) is inferior? Not necessarily. If n is sufficiently large then equation (1.2) covers all different categories of capital and all different categories of labor rather than using two gross variables K and L. Variation in factor augmentation rate of, say capital in (1.8), actually means that percentage of different types of capital has changed from one year to the next. What is explained in (1.8) as factor augmentation rate of capital would be reflected in (1.2) as change in factor shares of different categories of capital.

Thus alternative ways of studying productivity do not necessarily have to yield contradictory results. However they do not have to yield identical results either. Even if alternative models seem compatible at the root, differences will remain due to reasons such as variations in the methods of aggregation, or differences in the statistical estimation methods employed. The key is to be aware of different research works and their methodologies.

To have a comprehensive view of current research, the reader would benefit from also studying other recent works such as Allen and Diewert (1981), Banker, Charnes, Cooper and Schinnar (1981), Bergson (1981), the papers collected in the volume by Berndt and Field (1981), Bernhardt (1981), Boyer and Petit (1981), Christensen, Cummings and Schoech (1980), Denison (1979), Diewert (1979), the papers collected in Dogramaci (1981), Dogramaci and Adam (1981), Färe, Lovell and Zieschang (1982), Gold (1979, 1981), Jorgenson, Christensen and Cummings (1981), Gollop and Jorgenson (1980), Gollop and Roberts (1981a, 1981b), Jorgenson and Fraumeni (1980), Jorgenson (1981), Kendrick and Grossman (1980), the papers collected in Kendrick and Vaccara (1980), Cowing and Stevenson (1981), Leibenstein (1982), Mansfield (1980, 1981), Melman (1983), Nelson (1981), Page (1980), Schluter and Beeson (1981), and Shephard and Färe (1980).

Note

[1]As a simplistic but illustrative example, consider productivity of farming on a narrow but long strip of land of length L. (We choose this long and thin rectangular shape so that the discussion may be limited to a unidimensional context.) Assume that the fertility of soil

increases from one end of the strip to the other. Let t denote the position of any point throughout the length of the strip.: t = 0 is one end of the strip and t = L is the other end. Now, if we use a production function with two inputs, capital (farm machinery etc.) and labor, then equation (1) would indicate the total factor productivity change rates along this strip of land. However, if data are not available on continuous form, and we only have aggregate data from different plots of land along the strip, we would then replace the derivatives with finite differences in order to accommodate the discrete nature of the data.

References

Abramovitz, M., 1956, "Resources and Output Trends in the United States Since 1870," *American Economic Review* 46, no. 2:5–23.

Afriat, S., 1972, "Efficiency Estimation of Production Functions," *International Economic Review* 13:568–598.

Aigner, D. J.; T. Amemiya; and D. J. Poirier, 1976, "On the Estimation of Production Frontiers," *International Economic Review* 17:377–396.

Aigner, D. J., and S. F. Chu, 1968, "On Estimating the Industry Production Function," *American Economic Review* 58, no. 4:826–839.

Aigner, D. J., and P. J. Schmidt, eds., 1980, "Specification and Estimation of Frontier Production Profit and Cost Functions," *Annals of Applied Econometrics, 1980,* 2, *Journal of Econometrics* 13.

Aigner, D. J.; C. A. K. Lovell; and P. J. Schmidt, 1977, "Formulation and estimation of Stochastic Frontier Production function Models," *Journal of Econometrics* 6, no. 1:21–37.

Allen, R. C., and W. E. Diewert, 1981, "Direct versus Implicit Superlative Index Number Formulae," *Review of Economics and Statistics* 63, no. 3:430–435.

Banker, R. D.; A. Charnes; W. W. Cooper; and A. Schinnar, 1981, "A Bi-Extremal Principle for Frontier Estimation and Efficiency Evaluations," *Management Science* 27, no. 12:1370–1382.

Bergson, A., 1981, "Soviet Technological Progress: Trends and Prospects," Harvard Institute of Economic Research, Discussion Paper No. 814, February.

Berndt, E. 1980. "Comment on a paper by Gollop and Jorgenson" in New Developments in Productivity Measurement and Analysis, J. W. Kendrick and B. N. Vaccara, editors, NBER, Studies in Income and Wealth, vol 44, Chicago: University of Chicago Press, 124–136.

Berndt, E. R. and B. C. Field (eds.), 1981, *Modelling and Measuring Natural Resource Substitution*, Cambridge, MA: MIT Press.

Berndt, E. and M. Khaled, 1979, "Parametric Productivity Measurement and Choice of Flexible Functional Forms", Journal of Political Economy, vol. 87, no. 61, pp. 1220–1245.

Bernhardt, I., 1981, "Sources of Productivity Differences Among Canadian Manufacturing Industries," *Review of Economics and Statistics* 63, no. 4:503–512.

Boyer, R., and P. Petit, 1981, "Employment and Productivity in the EEC," *Cambridge Journal of Economics* 5:47–58.

Caves, D. W.; L. R. Christensen; and J. A. Swanson, 1981. "Productivity Growth, Scale Economies and Capacity Utilization in U.S. Railroads, 1955–74," *American Economic Review* 71, no. 5:994–1002.

Christensen, L. R.; D. Cummings; and P. E. Schoech, 1980, "Econometric Estimation of Scale Economies in Telecommunications," SSRI Workshop Series no. 8013, University of Wisconsin, Madison.

Christensen, L. R., and W. Greene, 1976, "Economies of Scale in U.S. Electric Power Generation," *Journal of Political Economy* 84, no. 4:655–767.

Cowing, T. G. and R. E. Stevenson, (eds.), 1981, *Productivity Measurement in Regulated Industries*, New York: Academic Press.

Denison, E. F., 1962, "Sources of Economic Growth in the U.S. and the Alternatives Before Us," Supplementary paper 13 (Washington D.C.: Committee for Economic Development).

Denison, E. F., 1979, *Accounting for Slower Economic Growth: The United States in the 1970's* (Washington, D.C.: Brookings Institution).

Denny, M.; M. Fuss; and J. D. May, 1981, "Intertemporal Changes in Regional Productivity in Canadian Manufacturing," *Canadian Journal of Economics* 14:390–408.

Diamond, P., and D. McFadden, 1965, "Identification of the Elasticity of Substitution and Bias of Technical Change: An Impossibility Theorem," mimeographed (Berkeley: University of California).

Diamond, P.; D. McFadden; and M. Rodriguez, 1978, "Measurement of the Elasticity of Factor Substitution and Bias of Technical Change," in Fuss and McFadden, vol. 2.

Diewert, W. E., 1971, "An Application of the Shephard Duality Theorem: A Generalized Leontief Production Function," *Journal of Political Economy*, vol. 79:481–507.

Dogramaci, A., ed., 1981, *Productivity Analysis: A Range of Perspectives* (Boston: Martinus Nijhoff Publishing).

Dogramaci, A., and N. R. Adam, eds., 1981. *Aggregate and Industry Level Productivity Analyses* (Boston: Martinus Nijhoff Publishing).

Färe, R., and V. Lyon, 1981, "The Determinateness Test and Economic Price Indices," *Económetrica vol* 49, no. 1:209–213.

Färe, R., C. A. K. Lovell and K. Zieschang. 1982. "Measuring the Technical Efficiency of Multiple Output Production Technologies," in Natural Resources and Production, edited by W. Eichorn, R. Henn, K. Neumann and R. Shephard, Wurzburg: Physica-Verlag.

Farrell, M. J., 1957, "The Measurement of Productive Efficiency," *Journal of The Royal Statistical Society*, A, 125, pt. 2:252–267.

Førsund, F. R., and L. Hjalmarsson, 1974, "On the Measurement of Productive Efficiency," *Swedish Journal of Economics* 76, no. 2:141–154.

Førsund, F. R., and L. Hjalmarsson, 1979, "Frontier Production Functions and Technical Progress: A Study of General Milk Processing in Swedish Dairy Plants," *Econometrica* 47, no. 4:883–900.

Førsund, F. R., and E. S. Jansen, 1977, "On Estimating Average and Best Practice Homothetic Production Functions via Cost Functions," *International Economic Review* 18, no. 2:463–476.

Fuss, M., and D. McFadden, eds., 1978, *Production Economics: A Dual Approach to Theory and Applications,* 2 vols. (Amsterdam: North-Holland).

Gold, B., 1979, *Productivity, Technology and Capital* (Lexington Mass.: Heath, Lexington Books).

Gold, B., 1981, "Changing Perspectives on Size, Scale, and Returns: An Interpretive Survey," *Journal of Economic Literature* 19, no. 1:5–33.

Gollop, F. M., 1979, "Accounting for Intermediate Input: The Link Between Sectoral and Aggregate Measures of Productivity Growth," in *Measurement and Interpretation of Productivity*, A. Rees and J. W. Kendrick (eds.), Washington D.C.: National Academy of Sciences

Gollop, F. M. and D. W. Jorgenson. 1980. "U.S. Productivity Growth by Industry, 1947–73" in New Developments in Productivity Measurement and Analysis, edited by J. W. Kendrick and B. N. Vaccara, Studies in Income and Wealth, vol 44, National Bureau of Economic Research, Chicago: The University of Chicago Press.

Gollop, F. M., and M. J. Roberts, 1981a, "The Sources of Growth in the U.S. Electric Power Industry" in *Productivity Measurement in Regulated Industries,* T. G. Cowing and R. E. Stevenson (eds.), New York: Academic Press.

Gollop, F. M. and M. J. Roberts. 1981b. "Imported Intermediate Input: Impact on Sectoral Productivity in U.S. Manufacturing," in Aggregate and Industry Level Productivity Analyses, edited by A. Dogramaci and N. R. Adam, Studies in Productivity Analysis, vol. 2, Boston: Martinus Nijhoff Publishing Co.

Greene, W. H. 1980, "Maximum Likelihood Estimation of Econometric Frontier Functions," *Journal of Econometrics* 13:27–56.

Griliches, Z., 1980, "R & D and the Productivity Slowdown," *American Economic Review* 70, no. 2:343–348.

Griliches, Z., and D. J. Jorgenson, 1966, "Sources of Measured Productivity Change: Capital Input," *American Economic Review* 56, no. 2:50–61.

Johansen, L., 1972, *Production Functions*, (Amsterdam: North Holland).

Jorgenson, D. W., 1981, "Energy Prices and Productivity Growth," in J. M. Rosow, ed., *Productivity Prospects for Growth* (New York: Van Nostrand Reinhold).

Jorgenson, D. W., and B. M. Fraumeni, 1980, "Relative Prices and Technical Change," Harvard Institute of Economic Research, Discussion Paper no. 752, December.

Jorgenson, D. W.; L. Christensen; and D. Cummings, 1981, "Relative Productivity Levels," *European Economic Review* vol. 13, no. 1.

Jorgenson, D. W. and Z. Griliches. 1967. "The Explanation of Productivity Change" Review of Economic Studies, vol. 34, no. 99 pp. 249–283.

Kendrick, J. W., 1956, "Productivity Trends: Capital and Labor," *Review of Economics and Statistics* 38, no. 3:248–257.

Kendrick, J. W., and E. Grossman, 1980, *Productivity in the United States: Trends and Cycles* (Baltimore: Johns Hopkins Press).

Kendrick, J. W., and B. N. Vaccara, eds., 1980, "New Developments in Productivity

Measurement and Anaysis," National Bureau of Economic Research, *Studies in Income and Wealth,* vol. 41 (Chicago: University of Chicago Press).

Kopp, R. J., 1981, "The Measurement of Productive Efficiency: A Reconsideration," *Quarterly Journal of Economics* 90, no. 3:477–503.

Leibenstein, H., 1982, "The Prisoner's Dilemma in the Invisible Hand: An Analysis of Productivity Growth Within The Firm" *American Economic Review* 72, no. 2:92–97.

Mansfield, E., 1980, "Basic Research and Productivity Increase in Manufacturing," *American Economic Review* 70:863–873.

Mansfield, E., 1981, "Composition of R & D Expenditures: Relationship to Size of Firm, Concentration and Innovative Output," *Review of Economics and Statistics* 63, no. 4:610–613.

Meeusen, W., and J. van den Broeck, 1977a, "Efficiency Estimation from Cobb-Douglas Production Functions with Composed Error," *International Economic Review* 18, no. 2:435–444.

Meeusen, W., and J. van den Broeck, 1977b, "Technical Efficiency and Dimension of The Firm: Some Results on the Use of Frontier Production Functions," *Empirical Economics* 2, no. 2:109–122.

Melman, S., 1983 (forthcoming), *Profits Without Production* (New York: Knopf).

Nadiri, M. I., and M. A. Schankerman, 1981, "Technical Change, Returns to Scale, and the Productivity Slowdown," *American Economic Review* 71, no. 2:314–319.

Nelson, R. R., 1981, "Research on Productivity Growth and Productivity Differences: Dead Ends and New Departures," *Journal of Economic Literature* 19, no. 3:1029–1064.

Ohta, M., 1974, "A Note on the Duality Between Production and Cost Functions: Rate of Returns to Scale and Rate of Technical Progress," *Economic Studies Quarterly* 25, December:63–65.

Page, J. M., Jr., 1980, "Technical Efficiency and Economic Performance: Some Evidence from Ghana," *Oxford Economic Papers* n.s., 32, no. 2:319–339.

Sato, K., 1975, *Production Functions and Aggregation* (Amsterdam: North-Holland).

Sato, R., 1970, "The Estimation of Biased Technical Progress and the Production Function," *International Economic Review* 11:179–208.

Sato, R., 1980, "The Impact of Technical Change on the Holothecity of Production Functions," *Review of Economic Studies* 47:767–776.

Sato, R., 1981, *Theory of Technical Change and Economic Invariance: Application of Lie Groups* (New York: Academic Press).

Schluter, G., and P. Beeson, 1981, "Components of Labor Productivity Growth in the Food System, 1958–67," *Review of Economics and Statistics* 63, no. 3:378–384.

Schmidt, P. J., 1978, "On the Statistical Estimation of Parametric Frontier Production Functions: A Rejoinder," *Review of Economics and Statistics* 58, no. 2:238–239.

Schmidt, P. J., 1978, "On the Statistical Estimation of Parametric Frontier Production Functions: A Rejoinder," *Review of Economics and Statistics* 60, no. 3:481–482.

Schmidt, P. J., and C. A. K. Lovell, 1979, "Estimating Technical and Allocative Inefficiency Relative to Stochastic Production and Cost Frontiers," *Journal of Econometrics* 9, no. 3:343–366.

Shephard, R. W., 1953, *Cost and Production Functions* (Princeton: Princeton University Press).

Shephard, R. W., 1970, *Theory of Cost and Production Functions* (Princeton: Princeton University press).

Shephard, R. W., and R. Färe, 1980, *Dynamic Theory of Production Correspondences* (Cambridge, Mass.: Oelgeschlager, Gunn & Hain Publishers).

Solow, R. M., 1957, "Technical Change and the Aggregate Production Function," *Review of Economics and Statistics* 39:312–320.

Solow, R. M., 1961, "Comment on Stigler's Paper, in Output, Input and Productivity Measurement," *Studies in Income and Wealth,* vol 25, National Bureau of Economic Research (Princeton: Princeton University Press), pp. 64–67, and 68–69.

Stevenson, R., 1980, "Measuring Technological Bias," *Amerian Economic Review* 70, no. 1:162–173.

Stigler, G. 1961, "Economic Problems in Measuring Changes in Productivity," in "Output, Input, and Productivity Measurement," *Studies in Income and Wealth,* vol. 25, National Bureau of Economic Research (Princeton: Princeton University Press).

Timmer, C. P., 1971, "Using a Probabilistic Frontier Production Function to Measure Technical Efficiency," *Journal of Political Economy* 79, no. 4:776–794.

Tinbergen, J., 1942, "Zur Theorie der Langfristigen Wirtschaftsentwicklung," *Weltwirtsschaftliches Archiv* 55, no. 1:511–549; translated as "On the Theory of Trend Movements," in L. H. Klassen, L. M. Koych, and H. J. Witteveen, eds. *Jan Tinbergen Selected Papers*, (Amsterdam: North-Holland, 1959), pp. 182–221.

Toda, Y., 1976, "Estimation of a Cost Function When Cost is not Minimum: The Case of Soviet Manufacturing Industries 1958–71," *Review of Economics and Statistics* 58, no. 3:259–268.

Uzawa, H., 1964, "Duality Principles in the Theory of Cost and Production," *International Economic Review,* vol. 5, pp.216–220.

2 Intertemporal Changes in the Levels of Regional Labor Productivity in Canadian Manufacturing

M. Denny and M. Fuss

2.1. Introduction

The relative economic efficiency and, consequently, the competitiveness of Canada's economic regions have been a source of dispute and political controversy since Confederation in 1867. In this paper we will present some empirical evidence on the levels and changes in regional efficiency in Canadian manufacturing. Due to data limitations, the nation is divided into five geographic regions. Three of these are the larger provinces; Quebec, Ontario, and British Columbia. The Atlantic region includes the four provinces on the east coast and the Prairie region incorporates the three remaining provinces. For the years 1961–1977 we have calculated the levels of regional efficiency in total manufacturing and for 1961–75 in the SIC two-digit manufacturing industries.

The methodology underlying the comparison was originally developed by Jorgenson and Nishimizu (1978). It has been extended by Denny and Fuss

Research assistance was provided by John Veitch, and Esther and Betty Chua. Early funding for data development came from the Ontario Ministry of Industry and Tourism and the SSHRC.

(1980) and Caves, Christensen, and Diewert (1980). In this particular application, we are focussing on the levels and changes in labor productivity. The regional level of regional labor productivity depends on two broad components. The first one is the level of total factor productivity and the second is the level of factor intensity. The latter is a weighted average of the quantitites of other inputs used per unit of labor.

Our findings confirm that there are large differentials in the labor productivity level differentials across the five regions. Quebec and the Atlantic region have labor productivity levels below, and the Prairies and British Columbia above Ontario. However, the differences in labor productivity levels are not predominantly differences in total factor productivity levels. The differences in the latter are in the same direction but average only approximately one-quarter of the differentials in labor productivity. Most of the labor productivity differentials are due to factor intensity differentials.

Over time, productivity has grown in all regions and the distribution of regional productivity growth has led to some shifts in the relative productivity levels. In general, all regions have benefitted and there is no evidence that large general shifts in relative labor productivity levels have occurred. The initial differences in total factor productivity have tended to remain throughout the period. There are more shifts in labor productivity and these are due to shifts in the factor intensity level.

The 1970s have seen massive downward shifts in the rate of growth of TFP. In many cases this has not led to declines in the growth of labor productivity. Increasing rates of growth of factor intensities have often more than offset the declines in total factor productivity growth.

2.2. A Conceptual Framework for Interregional and Intertemporal Productivity Comparisons

In this section we summarize the framework, developed in detail in Denny and Fuss (1980), for comparing productivity levels over time within a particular region, and productivity levels across regions at a particular point in time.[1]

Suppose the production process in region i at time t can be represented by the production function,

$$Q_{it} = F_{it}(X_{it}, T_{it}) \tag{2–1}$$

where Q_{it} is the output level $\{X_{it}\}$ is a vector of factor inputs, and T_{it} is an index of the technology; all in region i at time t. The logarithm of the production function F_{it} will be approximated by a quadratic function in the logarithms of X_{it}, T_{it}, and D. D is a vector (D_i) of dummy variables, one for every region other than a reference region. The approximation may be written

$$\log Q_{it} = F(\log X_{it}, \log T_{it}, D) \tag{2–2}$$

where F is a quadratic function. The approximation assumes that the production function in each region has common elements since we have replaced the function F_{it} in (2–1) with F in (2–2). Differences in regional production functions are maintained by the additional argument D in the production function, which has the effect of permitting constant and linear terms in the quadratic approximation to differ across regions.

Suppose that we wanted to know the difference between the level of output in region i at time s, and in region o at time t. Since the logarithmic production function is quadratic, we can apply Diewert's (1976) quadratic lemma to obtain

$$\begin{aligned}\Delta \log Q &= \log Q_{is} - \log Q_{ot} \\ &= \frac{1}{2}\left[\frac{\partial F}{\partial D_i}\bigg|_i + \frac{\partial F}{\partial D_i}\bigg|_o\right] \cdot [D_i - D_o] \\ &\quad + \frac{1}{2}\sum_k \left[\frac{\partial F}{\partial \log X_k}\bigg|_{X_k = X_{kis}} + \frac{\partial F}{\partial \log X_k}\bigg|_{X_k = X_{kot}}\right] \\ &\quad \times \{\log X_{kis} - \log X_{kot}] \\ &\quad + \frac{1}{2}\left[\frac{\partial F}{\partial \log T}\bigg|_{T=T_{is}} + \frac{\partial F}{\partial \log T}\bigg|_{T=T_{ot}}\right] \\ &\quad \times [\log T_{is} - \log T_{ot}]\end{aligned} \tag{2–3}$$

where $D_o = 0$. The output differential across regions and time periods may be broken down into the three terms in (2–3); a regional effect, an input effect, and an intertemporal effect. Define the regional effect as

$$\theta_{io} = \frac{1}{2}\left[\frac{\partial F}{\partial D_i}\bigg|_i + \frac{\partial F}{\partial D_i}\bigg|_o\right] \times [D_i - D_o] \tag{2–4}$$

and the intertemporal effect as

$$\mu_{io} = \frac{1}{2}\left[\frac{\partial F}{\partial \log T}\bigg|_{T=T_{is}} + \frac{\partial F}{\partial \log T}\bigg|_{T=T_{io}}\right] \times [\log T_{is} - \log T_{io}] \quad (2\text{–}5)$$

Constant returns to scale and perfect competition in input and output markets implies that $\partial F/(\partial \log X_k) = S_k$, the kth input's cost (value) share. Using these assumptions, we can rewrite (2–3) as

$$\Delta \log Q = \tfrac{1}{2} \sum_k [S_{kis} + S_{kot}]\,[\log X_{kis} + \log X_{kot}] + \theta_{io} + \mu_{io} \quad (2\text{–}6)$$

Suppose $k = L$ indexes the labor input (L). Then, using the fact that $\Sigma_k S_{kis} = \Sigma_k S_{kot} = 1$, equation (2–6) can be rewritten as

$$\Delta \log \frac{Q}{L} = \frac{1}{2} \sum_{k \neq L} [S_{kis} + S_{kot}] \left[\log \frac{X_{kis}}{L_{is}} - \log \frac{X_{kot}}{L_{ot}}\right] + \theta_{io} + \mu_{io} \quad (2\text{–}7)$$

The difference in labor productivity can be decomposed into three effects: (1) a factor intensity effect ($\log X/L$); (2) a regional effect (θ_{io}); and (3) an intertemporal effect (μ_{io}).

If we want to make an intertemporal comparison within one region, for example the reference region, then $D_i = D_o = 0$ and $s = t + 1$. Equation (2–7) becomes

$$\Delta \log \frac{Q}{L} = \frac{1}{2} \sum_{k \neq L} [S_{k,t+1} + S_{k,t}] \left[\log \frac{X_{k,t+1}}{L_{t+1}} - \log \frac{X_{k,t}}{L_t}\right] + \mu_{oo} \quad (2\text{–}8)$$

Define $\mu_{oo} \equiv \mu_{t,t+1}$ and rearrange (2–8) as

$$\mu_{t,t+1} = \left[\log\left(\frac{Q}{L}\right)_{t+1} - \log\left(\frac{Q}{L}\right)_t\right] - \frac{1}{2} \sum_{k \neq L} [S_{k,t+1} + S_{k,t}] \times \left[\log \frac{X_{k,t+1}}{L_t} - \log \frac{X_{k,t}}{L_t}\right] \quad (2\text{–}9)$$

The expression, $\mu_{t,t+1}$, is the Tornquist approximation to the rate of growth of productivity due to technical change for a particular region over time. Under our assumptions it is equal to the rate of growth of total factor productivity (TFP). The regional rate of growth of labor productivity equals the growth in TFP plus the growth in factor intensity, the last term in (2–9).

Alternatively, our general expression (2–7) can be specialized to make a comparison of the efficiency levels across regions at a point in time ($t = s$) in terms of relative labor productivities.

$$\theta_{io} = \left[\log\left(\frac{Q}{L}\right)_i - \log\left(\frac{Q}{L}\right)_o\right]$$

$$-\frac{1}{2}\sum_{k\neq L}[S_{ki} + S_{ko}]\left[\log\frac{X_{ki}}{L_i} - \log\frac{X_{ko}}{L_o}\right] \qquad (2\text{–}10)$$

Equation (2–10) can be used to measure the differences in regional efficiency in Canadian two-digit manufacturing. Differences in the *level* of labor productivity can be attributed to two broad components. The first one is the difference, θ_{io}, in the level of TFP, and the second is the weighted sum of differences in the level of factor intensities $\log(X_{ki}/L_i) - \log(X_{ko}/L_o)$.

The next section will provide a brief verbal summary of the technical material surveyed in this section.

2.3. Interpreting Labor Productivity Growth

Labor productivity is the most widely used and understood productivity measure. The ease with which it can be calculated contributes to its popularity. Underlying the changes in labor productivity are a number of distinctly different phenomena, and it will clarify the development prospects for manufacturing if we provide a breakdown of labor productivity into its major underlying components.

There are *two* broad components that contribute to any observed changes in labor productivity. First, the quantity of output that can be produced with any fixed bundle of labor, capital, and materials may increase. This improvement in the use of resources we will call the growth in *total factor productivity* (TFP). It is the first major component underlying labor productivity growth.

The second major component will be called changes in *factor intensities.* If the ratios of capital to labor and materials to labor change, then labor productivity will change. Increases in these ratios will raise labor productivity. There may be many reasons why factor intensities change. Shifts in relative prices, new technologies, and changes in the degree of processing are three major possibilities.

The two major components are not independent but they are of different significance. Changes in *factor intensities* may occur without any improvements in our ability to produce goods in a particular industry. In particular, they may occur without any increases in *TFP.* We will suggest that increases in labor productivity that are due to increases in *factor intensities* are qualitatively, although not quantitatively, less significant than increases in *TFP*.[2] As *TFP* grows, *factor intensities* may or may not change. It is clear that with TFP growth, in contrast with factor intensity growth, our capabilities of producing more with the same resources have improved.

The particular choice of our measure of relative efficiency levels is based on several requirements. First, we want to use observations on prices and quantities of inputs and outputs. Second, we do not want to either estimate or have prior knowledge of the parameters of the production function. The choice of a quadratic function and the use of quadratic lemma are crucial if these requirements are to be satisfied. The use of the quadratic function assures us, through the quadratic lemma, that we can *exactly* express, equation (2–3), changes in output in terms of only first-order derivatives of the function. For any nonquadratic case, one would have second-order derivatives in equation (2–5). It is not possible to know the value of these second-order derivatives with only price and quantity data. Consequently, it is fundamental that only first-order derivatives appear in (2–3). The latter derivatives can, under certain assumptions, be expressed in terms of price and quantity data. In summary, the quadratic assumption can not be eliminated without much more extensive data requirements. One could, in principle, change from the logarithmic case; but we have found it difficult to find practical alternatives that permit the calculation to be carried through. Finally, one cannot eliminate the assumption that the production functions are *not* totally different. All productivity analysis requires this restriction implicitly or explicitly.

2.4. Trends in Labor Productivity

The recent trends in the growth of labor productivity in Canadian manufacturing can be surveyed with the summary results shown in Table 2–1. For our five regions, this table shows the average annual rates of growth in labor productivity (col. 1) for three time periods, 1961–70, 1971–77, and, 1961–77. For the complete period, labor productivity grew fastest in Quebec followed closely by Ontario. British Columbia had the lowest labor productivity growth rate and the Prairies did only marginally better. The Atlantic region was substantially above the Western regions and substantially below the central regions.

Did the labor productivity growth rate rise or fall during the 1970s? It increased in Quebec, the Prairies, and the Atlantic region and fell in Ontario and British Columbia. The growth rate increases were 31%, 20%, and 13% in the Atlantic, Quebec, and Prairie regions, respectively. The decline in the

Table 2–1. Average Annual Rates of Growth of Productivity, in Regional Canadian Total Manufacturing

		Labor Productivity	*Factor Intensity*	*Total Factor Productivity*
Atlantic	1961–70	3.31	2.49	0.82
	1971–77	4.33	3.52	0.81
	1961–77	3.76	2.94	0.82
Quebec	1961–70	3.83	2.88	0.95
	1971–77	4.59	3.87	0.72
	1961–77	4.16	3.31	0.85
Ontario	1961–70	4.06	3.08	0.98
	1971–77	3.90	3.44	0.46
	1961–77	3.99	3.23	0.76
Prairies	1961–70	2.84	2.15	0.69
	1971–77	3.22	2.79	0.43
	1961–77	3.00	2.43	0.57
British Columbia	1961–70	3.06	2.09	0.97
	1971–77	2.51	2.22	0.29
	1961–77	2.82	2.15	0.67

growth rate equalled roughly 5% in Ontario and 15% in British Columbia. There was no uniform decline in the rate of growth of labor productivity in Canadian manufacturing during the 1970s.

The growth in labor productivity can be divided into growth in total factor productivity (Table 2–1, col. 3) and growth in the factor intensity (col. 2). There are several interesting patterns in this decomposition. First, the labor productivity growth rate is almost always composed of substantial growth in factor intensity. The latter is 60% to 75% of the growth in labor productivity. Second, in all regions the rate of growth of the factor intensity was higher in the 1970s relative to the 1960s. Third, in all regions the average TFP growth rate fell from the 1960s to the 1970s.

The net effect was an increase in the average labor productivity growth rate during the 1970s in three of the five regions and a decline in the other two. The Atlantic region had a very modest decline in the TFP growth rate offset by a large increase in the factor intensity growth. The growth rate of labor productivity increased sharply in the Atlantic region. A similar pattern occurred in Quebec and the Prairies. The declines in the labor productivity growth rates in Ontario and British Columbia were the result of very sharp declines in the TFP growth rate which were not entirely offset by modest increases in the factor intensity growth rate.

Underlying these broad patterns are more diverse changes in the rates of growth of outputs and inputs. In almost all regions the rate of growth of output slowed during the 1970s. Labor productivity continued to grow at relatively high rates because the growth in labor dropped more sharply than the growth in output.

Material inputs tend to grow at rates quite close to the output growth rate. In the 1970s the slowdown in output growth was accompanied by a slowdown in the rate of growth of material inputs. The rate of growth of capital inputs accelerated during the 1970s in contrast with labor or materials. The increased importance of the factor intensity growth rate component of labor productivity during the 1970s can be attributed to three phenomena. First, the capital to labor ratio was growing more rapidly in all regions. Second, the materials to labor ratio was growing more rapidly. The increase in this ratio was not as large as the capital–labor ratio. Third, the shares of material and capital relative to labor were rising, which tends to increase the rate of growth of the factor intensity component of the labor productivity decomposition. Certainly the major factor was the very rapid rate of growth of capital relative to labor and output.

2.5. Labor Productivity in Two-Digit Regional Manufacturing Industries

For the years 1961–75, we have collected the available data for the 20 industries at the 2-digit SIC level of regional manufacturing. For our five regions, we were able to construct complete data for 69 of the 100 possible cases. To maintain national industry coverage we have constructed a residual region, called the "Rest of Canada" for 11 industries in which a detailed regional breakdown was not possible. The Rest of Canada region includes the Atlantic and Prairie regions in all 11 cases. British Columbia is also included in 6 of the 11 cases.

The average rates of growth of labor productivity in each regional industry for 1961–75 are shown in Table 2–2. Suppose we compare the performance of industries in different regions. In which regions has the average labor productivity growth rate been relatively high? Ontario has the largest share of manufacturing industries and we will compare the rates of growth of labor productivity in each region with Ontario. To avoid judgements about rates of growth that are almost equal, a difference of at least 0.1% is required before any conclusions are drawn.[3] In the Rest of Canada, there has been a higher growth rate in 9 of 11 industries relative to Ontario. In seven of these industries, the growth rate difference was larger than one-half of a

Table 2–2. Average Annual Rates of Growth of Labor Productivity, 1961–75 (annual percentages)

Industries	*Atlantic*	*Quebec*	*Ontario*	*Prairies*	*British Columbia*	*Rest of Canada*
01 Food and Beverage	2.97	3.41	3.45	2.95	1.86	
02 Tobacco Products		2.08	4.71			
03 Rubber		4.08*	4.63			5.37
04 Leather		2.70	2.68			3.59
05 Textile	4.82	5.57	4.58	2.55	5.21	
06 Knitting Mills		6.47	5.15			6.10
07 Clothing		3.32	2.96		2.58	2.72
08 Wood	2.73	2.96	2.33	3.70	2.34	
09 Furniture	3.09	2.76	2.46	2.38	2.00	
10 Paper		2.65	1.97		2.53	3.08
11 Printing	3.25	3.42	2.12	2.09	2.41	
12 Primary Metals		1.83	1.86		2.28	3.86
13 Metallic Fabricating		2.82	3.24		2.60	3.60
14 Machinery		3.10	3.76	5.25	3.67	
15 Transportation		6.59	7.00		5.13	7.69
16 Electrical Products		3.30	4.13		3.65	4.19
17 Non-Metallic Minerals	3.52	3.43	2.15	2.86	2.30	
18 Petroleum and Coal		6.42	3.47			8.90
19 Chemical Products	2.76	4.84	4.20	4.71	4.09	
20 Miscellaneous		3.47*	3.62			1.98

*1963–1975.

percentage. For the Atlantic region, labor productivity has been growing at a higher rate than in Ontario for five of the seven industries for which comparisons can be made. The differences are larger than one-half a percentage in three of the industries. Contrasting Quebec and Ontario, the results are mixed. The rate of growth of labor productivity in Quebec has been higher for 10 of the 17 industries in which a significant difference occurred. In 12 of the 17 cases, the difference was at least one-half a percentage. In the seven industries that can be compared between Ontario and the Prairies, the latter had higher productivity growth in four industries. British Columbia is the only region in which productivity grew at a lower rate (7 of 12) in more industries than in Ontario. The evidence supports the conclusion that in most industries and for regions other than British Columbia, the rates of growth of labor productivity have been higher outside of Ontario. For example, for each of the 20 industries, which region has had the highest rate of growth? The Rest of Canada leads in eight industries, Quebec in five, Ontario in three, the Atlantic region and the Prairies in two each, and British Columbia in none. The lowest growth rates occurred in only one industry in the Atlantic region and one in the Rest of Canada; in six industries in Ontario and in Quebec, and in three industries in the Prairies and in British Columbia. Tempering the results from any ordinal ranking is the long period it takes for modest differences in *rates of growth* to close differences in *productivity levels.* For example, if one region was 20% less efficient in a particular industry at the beginning of our period, it would just catch up if productivity grew at an average rate that was 1% higher than in the other region.

The two major components of labor productivity growth—the growth in TFP and factor intensity growth—are shown in Tables 2–3 and 2–4 for the regional two-digit manufacturing industries. The detailed industry results can be summarized in a number of ways.

For the 20 industries, the highest rates of TFP growth occurred for five industries in each of Quebec, the Rest of Canada, and the Atlantic region; for none in Ontario; for one in the Prairies; and for four in British Columbia. Relative to the results for labor productivity, Ontario has done worse and British Columbia and the Atlantic region better. This is confirmed by the fact that the lowest rates were reported by nine Ontario industries, five Quebec industries, four Prairie industries, two British Columbia industries, and none in the Atlantic region and the Rest of Canada. Ontario industries were surpassed in TFP growth by seven of eight industries in the Rest of Canada, six of six industries in the Atlantic region, and twelve of eighteen cases in Quebec. Comparing TFP growth, the Prairie industries and Ontario were divided four to four. In British Columbia, TFP grew faster in seven out of ten industries relative to the same Ontario industry.

The highest rates of growth of factor intensity per industry occurred in six industries in Quebec and in the Rest of Canada, five in Ontario, two in the Prairies, one in the Atlantic region, and none in British Columbia. The lowest growth rates occurred in seven industries in British Columbia, five in Ontario, four in Quebec, two in the Prairies, and one in the Atlantic region and in the Rest of Canada.

Table 2–3. Average Annual Rates of Growth of Total Factor Productivity, 1961–75 (annual percentages)

Industries	*Atlantic*	*Quebec*	*Ontario*	*Prairies*	*British Columbia*	*Rest of Canada*
01 Food and Beverage	0.96	1.02	0.96	0.72	0.95	
02 Tobacco Products		1.02	0.87			
03 Rubber		1.68*	1.56			2.02
04 Leather		1.13	0.92			1.10
05 Textile	2.44	2.01	2.20	1.78	2.13	
06 Knitting Mills		2.17	2.21			2.29
07 Clothing		0.98	0.83		0.85	0.87
08 Wood	0.95	0.85	0.75	0.91	0.70	
09 Furniture	1.34	1.02	1.01	0.95	0.99	
10 Paper		0.93	0.80		1.04	0.81
11 Printing	1.71	1.36	1.09	1.42	1.56	
12 Primary Metals		0.91	1.05		1.64	1.10
13 Metallic Fabricating		1.14	1.34		1.41	1.20
14 Machinery		1.89	1.93	1.42	2.05	
15 Transportation		2.23	1.64		2.58	2.73
16 Electrical Products		1.14	1.55		1.67	1.69
17 Non-Metallic Minerals	1.54	1.28	1.13	1.19	0.91	
18 Petroleum and Coal		0.95	0.89			1.24
19 Chemical Products	2.57	2.26	2.34	2.68	2.32	
20 Miscellaneous		0.83*	0.22			0.22

*1963–1975.

The miserable performance by British Columbia in increasing labor productivity is entirely due to the very low rates of growth of factor intensity which eliminated the very good TFP performance in that region.

The extremely high levels of labor productivity growth in the Rest of Canada region was due to high rates of growth in both components. The Atlantic region's relatively modest rate of labor productivity growth was predominantly due to high TFP growth combined with lower factor intensity

Table 2–4. Average Annual Rates of Growth of Factor Intensity (annual percentages)

Industries	*Atlantic*	*Quebec*	*Ontario*	*Prairies*	*British Columbia*	*Rest of Canada*
01 Food and Beverage	2.01	2.39	2.49	2.23	0.91	
02 Tobacco Products		1.06	3.84			
03 Rubber		2.40*	3.07			3.35
04 Leather		1.57	1.76			2.49
05 Textile	2.38	3.56	2.38	0.77	3.08	
06 Knitting Mills		4.30	2.94			3.81
07 Clothing		2.34	2.13		1.73	1.85
08 Wood	1.82	2.11	1.58	2.79	1.64	
09 Furniture	1.75	1.74	1.45	1.43	1.01	
10 Paper		1.72	1.17		1.49	2.27
11 Printing	1.54	2.06	1.03	0.67	0.85	
12 Primary Metals		0.92	0.81		0.64	2.76
13 Metallic Fabricating		1.68	1.90		1.19	2.40
14 Machinery		1.21	1.83	3.83	1.62	
15 Transportation		4.36	5.36		2.55	4.96
16 Electrical Products		2.16	2.58		1.98	2.50
17 Non-Metallic Minerals	1.98	2.15	1.02	1.67	1.39	
18 Petroleum and Coal		5.47	2.58			7.66
19 Chemical Products	0.19	2.58	1.86	2.03	1.77	
20 Miscellaneous		2.64*	3.40			1.70

*1963–1975.

growth. The Prairies tended to have modest rates of growth of both components.

Ontario and Quebec are the only regions with all 20 industries represented. Quebec's labor productivity growth was superior to that of Ontario predominantly because TFP growth was higher in Quebec. Some Ontario industries had high rates of factor intensity growth and it was in these industries that Ontario's labor productivity was relatively high.

In summary, the Atlantic region and the Rest of Canada have had the highest rates of productivity growth in more industries than any other region using either productivity measure. Ontario industries have tended to be at the bottom. The largest difference between the rankings determined by the two measures occurs in British Columbia. Using labor productivity, British Columbia is tied with Ontario at the bottom. However, the region is only surpassed by the Atlantic region in TFP growth.

The differential rates of growth of productivity provide an incomplete description of the relative efficiency of Canadian regions. In the remainder of our paper, we will present some evidence on the relative levels of efficiency. These levels are crucially important to an understanding of the current problems in Canadian regional manufacturing. The differentials in the rates of growth can only be properly understood if we know the levels of productivity. The latter are required to understand whether regional differentials are closing or widening. In addition, the magnitude of the level differences are of major importance if a sensible description of the situation is to be made.

2.6. Differences in the Levels of Labor Productivity

Our results will be presented in a particular form that is relatively easy to understand. For the atemporal regional difference in regional labor productivity, rewrite equation (2–7).

$$\Delta \log \frac{Q}{L} = \frac{1}{2} \sum_{k \neq L} [S_{kis} + S_{kot}] \left[\log \frac{X_{kis}}{L_{is}} - \log \frac{X_{kot}}{L_{ot}} \right] + \theta_{io} \quad (2\text{–}11)$$

Define the aggregate logarithmic factor intensity differential,

$$\Delta \log (FI) = \frac{1}{2} \sum_{k \neq L} [S_{kis} + S_{kot}] \left[\log \frac{X_{kis}}{L_{is}} - \log \frac{X_{kot}}{L_{ot}} \right]$$

the relative total factor productivity level

$$TFP_{io} = \exp(\theta_{io}) \quad (2\text{–}12)$$

The relative labor productivity level is then given by

$$LP_{io} = TFP_{io} \cdot FI_{io} \quad (2\text{–}13)$$

where the relative aggregate factor intensity level is

$$FI_{io} = \exp[\Delta \log (FI)]$$

We will report results on the relative labor productivity levels, LP_{io}, and the relative total factor productivity levels, TFP_{io}.

The levels of labor productivity vary widely across Canada's regions. Table 2–5 (col. 1), shows the average level of labor productivity in each region relative to Ontario. The labor productivity level is substantially lower in the Atlantic and Quebec regions and higher in the Western regions than in Ontario. All regions, except the Atlantic region, had declines in their relative labor productivity level during the 1970s relative to the 1960s. For the Western regions there was a severe decline in the 1970s. The gain in the Atlantic region was modest.

The level of regional labor productivity depends on the quantities of materials and capital that are provided to the workforce. If we extract the contribution of differences in regional factor intensities to differences in labor productivity, what differences will be left? The answer is that relatively small differences remain. *The large differences in regional labor productivity levels are due to large differences in regional factor intensity levels.*

The removal of the differences in regional factor intensities leaves only the regional differences in TFP levels shown in Table 2.5 (col. 2). These differences are much smaller than the differences in regional labor productivity. Notice that the sharp declines in the labor productivity levels in the

Table 2–5. Regional Labor Productivity Levels Relative to Ontario in Canadian Total Manufacturing (Ontario = 100.0)

		Labor Productivity	*TFP*
Atlantic	1961–70	80.9	95.7
	1971–77	83.1	97.7
	1961–77	81.5	96.5
Quebec	1961–70	82.9	96.2
	1971–77	81.7	96.5
	1961–77	82.3	96.3
Ontario	1961–70	100.0	100.0
	1971–77	100.0	100.0
	1961–77	100.0	100.0
Prairies	1961–70	111.8	100.7
	1971–77	103.1	100.6
	1961–77	107.4	100.7
British Columbia	1961–70	111.8	102.8
	1971–77	98.7	101.8
	1961–77	105.9	102.3

two Western Canada regions was due to sharp declines in the relative factor intensity levels rather than the total factor productivity levels.

2.7. Labor Productivity Levels in Ontario and Quebec Two-Digit Industries

The results for five regions at the total manufacturing level will be supplemented in this section by a more detailed consideration of the 20 two-digit SIC industries in Ontario and Quebec. These two regions contain a very large share of the manufacturing establishments and are rivals for the large markets available in Eastern Canada.

Recall that in total manufacturing, these two regions had the highest rates of growth of labor productivity and factor intensity. Quebec had the highest rate of growth of TFP and Ontario was third behind the Atlantic region. In Ontario the *level* of labor productivity has roughly been 20% higher and the *level* of TFP 5% higher than in Quebec. Over 16 years, the growth rate advantage achieved by Quebec has been sufficiently small that much of the advantage held by Ontario at the beginning of the period remains at the end.

For the two-digit industries, the levels of labor productivity in Quebec relative to Ontario are shown in Table 2–6. There is a very wide dispersion in the average level of labor productivity. In one-half of the 20 industries, the average difference in levels is at least 15% and Ontario leads in seven of these. At the other extreme. in six industries, the labor productivity levels differ by 5% or less and Quebec leads in one-half of these. Ontario leads in the other four industries for a total of 14 of 20 industries in which Ontario's average labor productivity level is higher.

The results for the individual years support much the same conclusion. In each year, about half the industries have large differentials in labor productivity levels and Ontario's level is higher in about 70% of the industries. Underlying this static picture are some shifts in the relative performances of individual industries. In Table 2–7, the eleven industries with the largest intertemporal *changes* in relative labour productivity are listed. Quebec's labor productivity level has improved in eight industries in Ontario's in three. Of the eight Quebec industries, three were industries in which Quebec had an advantage at the beginning of the period. In one industry, Printing, Quebec had surpassed Ontario by the end of the period. The remaining four industries were ones in which Quebec's initial disadvantage was substantially reduced.

Table 2–6. Average Levels of Labor Productivity in Quebec Relative to Ontario by Two-Digit Industry (Ontario = 100)

Industries	*1961–75*	*1961–70*	*1971–75*
01 Food and Beverage	96	96	97
02 Tobacco Products	52	53	50
03 Rubber	78*	78*	78
04 Leather	85	86	83
05 Textile	91	86	83
06 Knitting Mills	117	114	123
07 Clothing	105	105	106
08 Wood	92	90	85
09 Furniture	87	89	85
10 Paper	105	103	107
11 Printing	101	99	104
12 Primary Metals	149	151	147
13 Metallic Fabricating	90	91	89
14 Machinery	69	67	72
15 Transportation	45	46	44
16 Electrical Products	97	103	87
17 Non-Metallic Minerals	94	93	95
18 Petroleum and Coal	246	215	303
19 Chemical Products	80	79	83
20 Miscellaneous	72*	71*	74

*Series begin in 1963.

Ontario overtook Quebec in only one industry, Electrical Products. For Ontario, our sample period was one in which some of its industries maintained their advantage but Quebec industries improved their performance in numerous cases.

The intertemporal shifts in labor productivity levels were predominantly the result of differential rates of growth in factor intensities and not total factor productivity shifts. There were only four industries in which the relative TFP level in Ontario and Quebec changed. The industries were Printing, Electrical Products, Miscellaneous Manufacturing Products, and Transportation Equipment.

The level of TFP in the Printing industry improved in Quebec, and this is consistent with the improvement in the labor productivity level. The level of TFP fell in the Quebec Electrical Products industry, and this is consistent with the decline in the labor productivity level. The improvement in Quebec's TFP level in Transportation Equipment and Miscellaneous

Table 2–7. Intertemporal Shifts in Labor Productivity Levels in Quebec Relative to Ontario Manufacturing, 1961–75

Quebec Improves	*Quebec Deteriorates*
05 Textile Products	09 Furniture
06 Knitting Mills	12 Primary Metals
08 Wood Products	16 Electrical Products
10 Paper and Allied Products	
11 Printing	
18 Petroleum and Coal Products	
19 Chemical Products	

Manufacturing Products did not result in an improved labor productivity level. In the remaining ten industries in which there was a shift in the labor productivity level, the shift must have been based entirely on changes in the relative factor intensity levels.

2.8. Summary

Our results support a conclusion that should not surprise economists but often seems to be ignored. All regions have benefited from increased productivity. There is no evidence of uniform major shifts in regional industrial productivity. The limited overall movements in relative efficiency suggest that the gaps may have been closing slightly during the first half of the 1970s relative to the 1960s.

While regional labor productivity levels differ sharply it is the factor intensity differentials that lead to these results. The levels of TFP do not differ markedly and have not changed significantly in most cases. Further investigation is required into the reasons for the sharp differentials in factor intensities. It is very unlikely that factor prices can explain these observations. A combination of variations in regional product lines and plant size may provide an important reason for these factor intensity differentials. If they do then it will be interesting to see how the relatively small TFP differentials are changed once further disaggregation is undertaken.

We intend to pursue these questions through a more detailed consideration of a number of specific industries and by using three-digit data in conjunction with the two-digit SIC data.

Notes

1. A less technical discussion of the framework is contained in the following section.

2. Consider the following example of the distinction we are making: Labor productivity will increase if we provide a worker with more capital. Unless there are improvements in the capital, this will be a change in factor intensity and not TFP.

3. This arbitrarily eliminates cases we believe to be insignificant because of data limitations combined with the very, very slow change in levels that would be implied by minor growth rate differences.

References

Caves, D.W.; L. Christensen; and E. Diewert, 1980, "Multi-lateral Comparisons of Output, Input and Productivity Using Superlative Index Numbers," SSRI, WP-8008 (revised) University of Wisconsin, Madison.

Denny, M., and M. Fuss, 1980, "Intertemporal and Interspatial Comparisons of Cost Efficiency and Productivity," IPA, WP #8018, University of Toronto, Toronto.

Denny, M.; M. Fuss; and J. D. May, 1981, "Intertemporal Changes in Regional Productivity in Canadian Manufacturing," *Canadian Journal of Economics* 14:390–408.

Diewert, W. E., 1976, "Exact and Superlative Index Numbers," *Journal of Econometrics* 4:115–145.

Jorgenson, D., and K. Nishimizu, 1978, "U.S. and Japanese Economic Growth, 1952–74: An International Comparison," *Economic Journal* 88:707–726.

3 GROWTH ACCOUNTING IN AN OPEN ECONOMY

F. M. Gollop

3.1. Introduction

The proper economic characterization of aggregate productivity growth depends on society's economic objective for production. Kuznets, Solow, Denison, and others analyzing aggregate productivity growth reason that goods destined for final demand are the ultimate objective of economic production. Kendrick (1973) presents the argument clearly:

> It is the final products included in national product that are the objective of production. These are the goods that satisfy current consumer wants or that add to stocks of productive capacity for satisfying future wants, to use the definition of Kuznets and many earlier national income theorists.[1]

The appropriate measure of aggregate output is the sum of sectoral deliveries to final demand.

Sectoral deliveries to intermediate demand are excluded from present aggregate productivity research because they are viewed as self-canceling transactions. Kendrick (1973) states the argument best:

> Inclusion of intermediate inputs obviously involves double counting, since such inputs have already been included in the final products and the factor services required to produce them are likewise included in total factor input.[2]

Given this characterization of economic activity, deliveries to final demand can be shown to equal national net output or, as conventionally described, aggregate value added.[3] The result is that studies of aggregate economic performance typically define productivity at the economy-wide level as the efficiency with which labor and capital inputs are converted into aggregate value added. For all their important differences, Solow (1957), Kendrick (1961, 1973), Denison (1962, 1974, 1979), Jorgenson and Griliches (1967), Christensen and Jorgenson (1973), and Kendrick and Grossman (1980) adopt this conventional approach to aggregate growth accounting.

This paper does not take issue with the above description of the economy's macroeconomic objective. Deliveries to final demand are certainly an economy's ultimate economic concern for production.[4]. What this paper does focus on is the implicit characterization of microeconomic activity, particularly the treatment of intermediate input and deliveries to intermediate demand. Their self-canceling property is neither an economic truism nor the result of any particular characterization of society's economic objective. It follows, instead, from the assumption that the economy is closed to trade in foreign-produced inputs.

The intuition underlying this proposition is straightforward. The domestic economy's intermediate input equals the sum of domestically produced intermediate goods *and* foreign-supplied materials. Total intermediate input purchases and domestic deliveries to intermediate demand are self-canceling transactions only in an economy importing no intermediate inputs.

The implications for modeling and measuring aggregate productivity growth are equally direct. For an economy closed to trade in imported inputs, intermediate input transactions can be viewed as internal, offsetting transfers. Incorporating them into a model of aggregate production unnecessarily involves doublecounting. Consequently, macroeconomic models can suppress the vertically interdependent structure of macroeconomic activity. The important result demonstrated in this paper is that, for an economy closed to foreign-produced materials, value-added and delivery-to-final-demand models produce equivalent measures of aggregate productivity growth. The models' distinctly different descriptions of macroeconomic objectives and characterizations of microeconomic activity and sectoral production simply are of no consequence. Once trade in foreign-supplied inputs is introduced, however, domestic deliveries to intermediate demand and intermediate input purchases by domestic sectors are neither internal nor offsetting transfers. The aggregate economy can be viewed neither as a composite of horizontally independent sectors nor as an entity independent of foreign producing sectors. Modeling aggregate productivity in terms of value added or deliveries to final demand now makes a difference. The important conclusion is that, for an economy importing material inputs, the final measure of aggregate productivity growth depends importantly on the initial descriptions of both the economy's macroeconomic objectives and the technical properties of microeconomic production.

Sections 3.2 and 3.3 of this paper contrast measures of aggregate productivity growth derived from value-added and delivery-to-final-demand models of economic activity. The value-added model is the subject of section 3.2. Its specific assumptions for sectoral production and microeconomic activity, implicit in most productivity research, are introduced explicitly into the model of aggregate production. Section 3.3 develops an analogous framework for a model of aggregate productivity based on deliveries to final demand. Again, the model's underlying assumptions regarding sectoral production and microeconomic transactions are introduced explicitly. The most important finding is that, for an economy open to trade in foreign-supplied materials, the value-added model results in a higher measure of aggregate productivity growth than does the model defined in terms of deliveries to final demand.

The remainder of the paper addresses the important implications of redefining aggregate productivity growth in an "open" economy framework. Section 3.4 derives the link between sectoral measures of productivity growth and the measure of aggregate productivity growth. Both intersectoral and international transactions are relevant. Section 3.5 completes the analysis with a discussion of the practical consequences of these findings for intertemporal and international productivity comparisons.

3.2. Value Added

The aggregate economy is a collection of vertically related, interdependent sectors. Each sector uses labor, capital, and intermediate inputs to produce products delivered to final and/or intermediate demands. There is certainly no requirement that intermediate input purchases by an individual sector exactly offset its deliveries to intermediate demand. Stated equivalently, there is no requirement that the net output (or value added) of any sector equal its deliveries to final demand. Still, for an economy closed to trade in foreign material inputs, domestic deliveries to intermediate demand and intermediate input purchases can be viewed as internal transfers that at the economy-wide level are self-canceling transactions. Labor and capital are the only primary inputs. Aggregate deliveries to final demand equal aggregate value added. The macro economy then can be viewed as a set of horizontally independent sectors, each producing value added from labor and capital inputs. This line of reasoning forms the basis for those studies of aggregate productivity that describe the economy's objectives in terms of deliveries to final demand yet model aggregate productivity growth and microeconomic production in terms of value added.

Modeling macroeconomic activity and aggregate productivity growth in terms of value added begins with defining aggregate value added as a proportion of all quantities of sectoral value added. The maximum value of aggregate value added (λ) then can be expressed as a function of all quantities of sectoral value added, the supplies of labor and capital inputs, and time:

$$\lambda = F(V_1, V_2, \ldots, V_n, L_{11}, L_{12}, \ldots, L_{rn}, K_{11}, K_{12}, \ldots, K_{sn}, t) \tag{3-1}$$

where

$V_j \equiv$ quantity of the jth sector's value added
$L_{lj} \equiv$ lth labor input used in the jth sector
$K_{kj} \equiv$ kth capital input used in the jth sector
$t \equiv$ an index of time

Society's economic problem is to maximize λ given linearly homogeneous value-added functions

$$V_j = V^j(L_{1j}, L_{2j}, \ldots, L_{rj}, K_{1j}, K_{2j}, \ldots, K_{sj}, t) \qquad (j = 1, 2, \ldots, n) \tag{3-2}$$

market equilibrium conditions, and supplies of labor and capital inputs.

The model of aggregate value added is characterized by constant returns to scale. This is required by the sectoral value-added functions which constrain the macroeconomic maximization problem. The function F is therefore homogeneous of degree minus one in the quantities of sectoral value added, homogeneous of degree one in the factor supplies, and homogeneous of degree zero in the quantities of value added and inputs. Taken together, these conditions imply:

$$\sum_j \frac{\partial \ln F}{\partial \ln V_j} = -1$$

$$\sum_j \sum_l \frac{\partial \ln F}{\partial \ln L_{lj}} + \sum_j \sum_k \frac{\partial \ln F}{\partial \ln K_{kj}} = 1$$

$$\sum_j \frac{\partial \ln F}{\partial \ln V_j} + \sum_j \sum_l \frac{\partial \ln F}{\partial \ln L_{lj}} + \sum_j \sum_k \frac{\partial \ln F}{\partial \ln K_{kj}} = 0 \qquad (3\text{–}3)$$

It is important to emphasize that the particular characterization of macroeconomic activity embodied in equation (3–1) has important technical implications for sectoral production. The existence of sectoral value-added functions V^j implies that sectoral production of gross output is characterized by value-added separability:

$$Z_j = f^j[V^j(L_{1j}, L_{2j}, \ldots, L_{rj}, K_{1j}, K_{2j}, \ldots, K_{sj}, t), X_{1j}, \ldots, X_{nj}] \qquad (j = 1, 2, \ldots, n) \qquad (3\text{–}4)$$

where

$Z_j \equiv$ gross output of the jth sector
$X_{ij} \equiv$ ith intermediate input used in the jth sector

Maintaining the separability of value added and intermediate inputs implies that the technical properties of V^j, including all the properties of technical change, can be analyzed in isolation from intermediate inputs. In particular, the marginal rate of substitution between any pair of labor and/or capital inputs is independent of the level and mix of intermediate inputs. In addition, intermediate inputs cannot be sources or mediums of productivity growth. If technical change occurs, it can affect output only through V^j. If technical change is of the factor-augmenting type, it can augment only capital and/or labor inputs. Neither Hicks-neutral nor Leontief-neutral technical change is possible in a sector characterized by value-added separability. Stated formally, intermediate inputs are excluded from a value-added model of macroeconomic activity not only because they are viewed as self-canceling transactions but also because they are considered unimportant to the analysis of underlying sectoral productivity growth.[5]

The expression for aggregate productivity growth follows directly both from the technical properties of macroeconomic and microeconomic production and from the necessary conditions for producer equilibrium. The measure of aggregate productivity growth is derived by first fixing the level of aggregate value added at unity:

$$1 = F(V_1, V_2, \ldots, V_n, L_{11}, L_{12}, \ldots, L_{rn}, K_{11}, K_{12}, \ldots, K_{sn}, t) \qquad (3\text{–}5)$$

This expression defines a production-possibilities frontier for the macro economy. Given this frontier, equilibrium conditions in a competitive economy require that the elasticities described in (3–3) equal value shares in aggregate value added:

$$\frac{\partial \ln F}{\partial \ln V_j} = \frac{-q_j^v V_j}{\sum_j q_j^v V_j} \qquad (j = 1, 2, \ldots, n)$$

$$\frac{\partial \ln F}{\partial \ln K_{kj}} = \frac{p_{lj} L_{lj}}{\sum_j q_j^v V_j} \qquad (l = 1, 2, \ldots, r;\ j = 1, 2, \ldots, n)$$

$$\frac{\partial \ln F}{\partial \ln K_{kj}} = \frac{p_{kj} K_{kj}}{\sum_j q_j^v V_j} \qquad (k = 1, 2, \ldots, s;\ j = 1, 2, \ldots, n) \qquad (3\text{–}6)$$

where q_j^v is the price of the quantity of value added in the jth sector, and p_{lj} and p_{kj} are the prices corresponding to the lth labor input and the kth capital input, respectively, in the jth sector.

The homogeneity conditions (3–3) and the equilibrium conditions (3–6) together require that the value shares satisfy the summation conditions:

$$\sum_j \frac{q_j^v V_j}{\sum_j q_j^v V_j} = 1 \qquad (3\text{–}7\text{a})$$

$$\sum_j \sum_l \frac{p_{lj} L_{lj}}{\sum_j q_j^v V_j} + \sum_j \sum_k \frac{p_{kj} K_{kj}}{\sum_j q_j^v V_j} = 1 \qquad (3\text{–}7\text{b})$$

Condition (3–7a) is true by construction. The value of aggregate value added equals the sum of all sectoral value added. Conditon (3–7b) follows from sectoral and aggregate accounting identities. Verifying (3–7b) begins with the sectoral accounting identity relating the value of total output and payments to all factors of production:

$$q_j Z_j = \sum_l p_{lj} L_{lj} + \sum_k p_{kj} K_{kj} + \sum_i p_i X_{ij} \qquad (j = 1, 2, \ldots, n) \quad (3\text{–}8)$$

where p_i is the price of the ith intermediate input.[6] The value of sectoral value added equals the value of output less the value of intermediate input purchases:

$$q_j^v V_j = q_j Z_j - \sum_i p_i X_{ij} \qquad (j = 1, 2, \ldots, n) \qquad (3\text{–}9)$$

Substituting (3–8) into (3–9) and summing over all n sectors yields

$$\sum_j q_j^v V_j = \sum_j \sum_l p_{lj} L_{lj} + \sum_j \sum_k p_{kj} K_{kj} \qquad (3\text{–}10)$$

establishing the result required by (3–7b).

An expression for the rate of aggregate productivity growth now can be derived from the production-possibilities frontier (3–5) and the conditions for producer equilibrium (3–6). The total logarithmic derivative of F with respect to time can be expressed in the form

$$0 = \sum_j \frac{\partial \ln F}{\partial \ln V_j} \frac{d \ln V_j}{dt} + \sum_j \sum_l \frac{\partial \ln F}{\partial \ln L_{lj}} \frac{d \ln L_{lj}}{dt} + \sum_j \sum_k \frac{\partial \ln F}{\partial \ln K_{kj}} \frac{d \ln K_{kj}}{dt} + \frac{\partial \ln F}{\partial t} \tag{3–11}$$

where $\partial \ln F/\partial t$ is the rate of aggregate productivity growth. Using the equilibrium conditions (3–6), the aggregate rate of productivity growth (E_v) can be expressed in the following form:

$$E_V \equiv \frac{\partial \ln F}{\partial t} = \sum_j \frac{q_j^v V_j}{\sum_j q_j^v V_j} \frac{d \ln V_j}{dt} - \sum_j \sum_l \frac{p_{lj} L_{lj}}{\sum_j q_j^v V_j} \frac{d \ln L_{lj}}{dt} - \sum_j \sum_k \frac{p_{kj} K_{kj}}{\sum_j q_j^v V_j} \frac{d \ln K_{kj}}{dt} \tag{3–12}$$

This result can be summarized as a familiar proposition.

Proposition 1. The rate of aggregate productivity growth for an economy maximizing net output (value added) is defined as the weighted average of rates of growth of sectoral value added (with weights equal to sectoral value added shares in aggregate net output) less the weighted average of rates of growth of labor and capital inputs (with weights equal to the value shares of input payments in aggregate net output). Both sets of weights sum to unity.

The expression (3–12) applies to all economies, whether open or closed to trade in foreign-produced inputs. Intermediate inputs, whether purchased from domestic or foreign producers, do not enter the production-possibilities frontier (3–5) or the sectoral value-added functions (3–2), nor do they influence the equilibrium conditions (3–6). The sectoral value-added functions (3–2) maintain that microeconomic and therefore macroeconomic production are characterized by value-added separability. This assumption maintains that *all* the properties of productivity growth, including its measurement, can be analyzed in isolation from the level and mix of intermediate inputs.

What is important to note is that the model of aggregate productivity stated in terms of value added does not depend on the assumption that domestic deliveries to intermediate demand and total intermediate input purchases are self-canceling transactions. It depends solely on the assumption of value-added separability. Not surprisingly, the resulting measure of aggregate productivity growth (3–12) is insensitive to the economy's external trade in foreign-produced intermediate goods.

3.3 Deliveries to Final Demand

A model of aggregate productivity growth stated in terms of deliveries to final demand is constrained by sectoral production functions, not sectoral value-added functions. Value-added separability is not a maintained hypothesis. Consequently, intersectoral *and* international transactions in material inputs are not suppressed. The vertical structure of the aggregate economy is recognized explicitly.

The model of economic activity defined in terms of deliveries to final demand not only accounts for material inputs but depends importantly on the sources of those inputs. Total deliveries to an economy's intermediate demand equal the sum of domestic and foreign deliveries. *Domestic* deliveries to intermediate demand are truly intermediate goods. They are produced from primary labor and capital inputs supplied to the domestic economy. *Foreign* deliveries to domestic intermediate demand are not intermediate goods from the perspective of the domestic economy. They are primary inputs to be treated symmetrically with the domestic economy's labor and capital inputs. Domestic deliveries to intermediate demand are purely internal, offsetting transfers in *intermediate* inputs. Foreign deliveries, in contrast, are wholly external transactions in *primary* inputs. It follows that the formal specification of an aggregate model defined in terms of the domestic economy's deliveries to final demand and its primary inputs differs depending on whether the economy is "open" or "closed" to trade in foreign-produced inputs. The two models are developed separately below. Their results are contrasted with the value-added model described in section 3.2.

The Closed Economy

Society's objective is to maximize aggregate output defined as deliveries to final demand. The maximum value of aggregate deliveries to final demand (μ) can be expressed as a function of all quantities of sectoral deliveries to final demand (Y_j), labor and capital inputs, and time:

$$\mu = G(Y_1, Y_2, \ldots, Y_n, L_{11}, L_{12}, \ldots, L_{rn}, K_{11}, K_{12}, \ldots, K_{sn}, t) \tag{3–13}$$

The model abstracts from intermediate inputs and sectoral deliveries to intermediate demand since, given the absence of any imported inputs, all domestic sales and purchases of intermediate inputs are self-canceling transactions.

The economy-wide maximization problem is constrained by the supplies of the primary inputs, labor and capital, and by linearly homogeneous sectoral production functions:

$$Z_j = g^j(L_{1j}, L_{2j}, \ldots, L_{rj}, K_{1j}, K_{2j}, \ldots, K_{sj}, X_{1j}, X_{2j}, \ldots, X_{nj}, t) \qquad (j = 1, 2, \ldots, n) \qquad (3\text{–}14)$$

It is important to note that all inputs are treated symmetrically in the sectoral production functions g^j, unlike the sectoral production functions (3–4) constraining the value-added model described in section 3.2. Value-added separability is not a maintained hypothesis. There are no restrictions either on the marginal rate of substitution between any pair of inputs or on the properties of technical change. Though intermediate inputs do not appear explicitly in the macro model (3–13), they enter the problem through the constraints (3–14). Microeconomic production for delivery to intermediate demand is an important part of the solution to the macroeconomic problem maximizing deliveries to final demand.

The aggregate function G exhibits constant returns to scale. It is homogeneous of degree minus one in sectoral deliveries to final demand, homogeneous of degree one in labor and capital inputs, and homogeneous of degree zero in final demand deliveries and all inputs:

$$\sum_j \frac{\partial \ln G}{\partial \ln Y_j} = -1$$

$$\sum_j \sum_l \frac{\partial \ln G}{\partial \ln L_{lj}} + \sum_j \sum_k \frac{\partial \ln G}{\partial \ln K_{kj}} = 1$$

$$\sum_i \frac{\partial \ln G}{\partial \ln Y_j} + \sum_j \sum_l \frac{\partial \ln G}{\partial \ln L_{lj}} + \sum_j \sum_k \frac{\partial \ln G}{\partial \ln K_{kj}} = 0 \qquad (3\text{–}15)$$

Forming the production-possibilities frontier

$$1 = G(Y_1, Y_2, \ldots, Y_n, L_{11}, L_{12}, \ldots, L_{rn}, K_{11}, K_{12}, \ldots, K_{sn}, t) \qquad (3\text{–}16)$$

necessary conditions for producer equilibrium require the following relations:

$$\frac{\partial \ln G}{\partial \ln Y_j} = \frac{-q_j^y\, Y_j}{\sum_j q_j^y\, Y_j} \qquad (j = 1, 2, \ldots, n)$$

$$\frac{\partial \ln G}{\partial \ln L_{lj}} = \frac{p_{lj}\, L_{lj}}{\sum_j q_j^y\, Y_j} \qquad (l = 1, 2, \ldots, r;\ j = 1, 2, \ldots, n)$$

$$\frac{\partial \ln G}{\partial \ln K_{kj}} = \frac{p_{kj}\, K_{kj}}{\sum_j q_j^y\, Y_j} \qquad (k = 1, 2, \ldots, s;\ j = 1, 2, \ldots, n) \tag{3–17}$$

where q_j^y *is the price of goods delivered to final demand in the* jth sector.

The homogeneity restrictions (3–15) and the equilibrium conditions (3–17) together require

$$\sum_j \frac{q_j^y\, Y_j}{\sum_j q_j^y\, Y_j} = 1 \tag{3–18a}$$

$$\sum_j \sum_l \frac{p_{lj}\, L_{lj}}{\sum_j q_j^y\, Y_j} + \sum_j \sum_k \frac{p_{kj}\, K_{kj}}{\sum_j q_j^y\, Y_j} = 1 \tag{3–18b}$$

Condition (3–18a) is true by construction. Condition (3–18b) follows directly from accounting identities relating the value of a sector's total production both to the sum of the values of that sector's deliveries to intermediate and final demands and to the sum of that sector's payments to all factors of production:[7]

$$q_j Z_j = \sum_i p_j X_{ji} + q_j^y\, Y_j \qquad (j = 1, 2, \ldots, n) \tag{3–19}$$

$$q_j Z_j = \sum_l p_{lj} L_{lj} + \sum_k p_{kj} K_{kj} + \sum_i p_i X_{ij} \quad (j = 1, 2, \ldots, n) \tag{3–20}$$

Summing (3–19) and (3–20) over all sectors and equating the results produces the condition required by (3–18b).

$$\sum_j q_j^y\, Y_j = \sum_j \sum_l p_{lj} L_{lj} + \sum_j \sum_k p_{kj} K_{kj} \tag{3–21}$$

since

$$\sum_j \sum_i p_j X_{ji} = \sum_j \sum_i p_i X_{ij}$$

The rate of aggregate productivity growth (E_y) now can be solved from the total logarithmic derivative of G with respect to time:

$$E_y \equiv \frac{\partial \ln G}{\partial t} = -\sum_j \frac{\partial \ln G}{\partial \ln Y_j} \frac{d \ln Y_j}{dt} - \sum_j \sum_l \frac{\partial \ln G}{\partial \ln L_{lj}} \frac{d \ln L_{lj}}{dt}$$

$$- \sum_j \sum_k \frac{\partial \ln G}{\partial \ln K_{kj}} \frac{d \ln K_{kj}}{dt} \tag{3-22}$$

so that, using equilibrium conditions (3–17),

$$E_y = \sum_j \frac{q_j^y \; Y_j}{\sum_j q_j^y \; Y_j} \frac{d \ln Y_j}{dt} - \sum_j \sum_l \frac{p_{lj} L_{lj}}{\sum_j q_j^y \; Y_j} \frac{d \ln L_{lj}}{dt}$$

$$- \sum_j \sum_k \frac{p_{kj} K_{kj}}{\sum_j q_j^y \; Y_j} \frac{d \ln K_{kj}}{dt} \tag{3-23}$$

The rate of aggregate productivity growth for a model stated in terms of deliveries to final demand can be expressed as the weighted average of the rates of growth of sectoral deliveries to final demand less a weighted average of rates of growth of labor and capital inputs.[8]

Distinctly different characterizations of macroeconomic objectives and microeconomic activity are modeled by the value-added and delivery-to-final-demand production-possibilities frontiers F and G defined, respectively, in (3–5) and (3–16). The frontier F is concerned with maximizing aggregate net output, is defined in terms of sectoral value added, and is based on value-added functions for each sector. The macro economy is viewed as a set of horizontally independent sectors. Intersectoral transactions are ignored. Value-added separability, with all its implications for sectoral and aggregate productivity growth, is a maintained assumption. In contrast, the frontier G is concerned with maximizing deliveries to economy-wide final demand, is stated in terms of sectoral deliveries to final demand, and is based on constant-returns-to-scale production functions for each producing sector. The macro economy is modeled as a collection of vertically interdependent sectors. An active market in intersectoral transactions is recognized explicitly.

In spite of these fundamental differences, the following proposition holds:

Proposition 2. For an economy *closed* to trade in foreign-produced inputs, value-added and delivery-to-final-demand models of macroeconomic production lead to identical measures of aggregate productivity growth.

The proposition asserts that the rate of aggregate productivity growth E_v defined in (3–12) equals the aggregate rate E_y defined in (3–23). Verifying this proposition *for a closed economy* is a straightforward exercise.

Consider first the accounting identities expressed in equations (3–9) and (3–19). The former defines the value of a sector's value added as the value of that sector's output less the value of its intermediate input purchases. The latter states that the value of each sector's output equals the sum of the values of its products delivered to intermediate and final demands. Totally differentiating (3–9) and (3–19) with respect to time leads to expressions that, respectively, can be written in the forms,

$$\frac{d \ln V_j}{dt} = \frac{q_j Z_j}{q_j^v V_j} \frac{d \ln Z_j}{dt} - \sum_i \frac{p_i X_{ij}}{q_j^v V_j} \frac{d \ln X_{ij}}{dt} \qquad (j = 1, 2, \ldots, n) \tag{3–24}$$

$$\frac{d \ln Z_j}{dt} = \sum_i \frac{p_j X_{ji}}{q_j Z_j} \frac{d \ln X_{ji}}{dt} + \frac{q_j^y Y_j}{q_j Z_j} \frac{d \ln Y_j}{dt} \qquad (j = 1, 2,, \ldots, n) \tag{3–25}$$

Substituting (3–25) into (3–24) and substituting the resulting expression for the growth of sectoral value added into equation (3–12), the expression for E_v, yields

$$E_v =$$

$$\sum_j \frac{q_j^v V_j}{\sum_j q_j^v V_j} \left[\frac{q_j Z_j}{q_j^v V_j} \left(\sum_i \frac{p_j X_{ji}}{q_j Z_j} \frac{d \ln X_{ji}}{dt} + \frac{q_j^y Y_j}{q_j Z_j} \frac{d \ln Y_j}{dt} \right) - \sum_i \frac{p_i X_{ij}}{q_j^v V_j} \frac{d \ln X_{ij}}{dt} \right]$$

$$- \sum_j \sum_l \frac{p_{lj} L_{lj}}{\sum_j q_j^v V_j} \frac{d \ln L_{lj}}{dt} - \sum_j \sum_k \frac{p_{kj} K_{kj}}{\sum_j q_j^v V_j} \frac{d \ln K_{kj}}{dt} = \sum_j \frac{q_j^y Y_j}{\sum_j q_j^v V_j} \frac{d \ln Y_j}{dt}$$

$$- \sum_j \sum_l \frac{p_{lj} L_{lj}}{\sum_j q_j^v V_j} \frac{d \ln L_{lj}}{dt} - \sum_j \sum_k \frac{p_{kj} K_{kj}}{\sum_j q_j^v V_j} \frac{d \ln K_{kj}}{dt} \tag{3–26}$$

since

$$\sum_j \sum_i \frac{p_j X_{ji}}{\sum_j q_j^v V_j} \frac{d \ln X_{ji}}{dt} = \sum_j \sum_i \frac{p_i X_{ij}}{\sum_j q_j^v V_j} \frac{d \ln X_{ij}}{dt}$$

Multiplying the expression for E_v in (3–26) by the ratio of the value of aggregate value added to the value of aggregate deliveries to final demand produces an expression identical to the definition of E_y in 3–23):

$$\frac{\sum_j q_j^v V_j}{\sum_j q_j^y Y_j} E_v = \sum_j \frac{q_j^y Y_j}{\sum_j q_j^y Y_j} \frac{d \ln Y_j}{dt} - \sum_j \sum_l \frac{p_{lj} L_{lj}}{\sum_j q_j^y Y_j} \frac{d \ln L_{lj}}{dt}$$

$$- \sum_j \sum_k \frac{p_{kj} K_{kj}}{\sum_j q_j^y Y_j} \frac{d \ln K_{kj}}{dt} \tag{3–27}$$

so that

$$E_v = \frac{\sum_j q_j^y Y_j}{\sum_j q_j^v V_j} E_y \tag{3–28}$$

Finally, consider the accounting relation in a closed economy between the values of aggregate value added and aggregate deliveries to final demand. As defined in (3–9), the value of sectoral value added equals the value of sectoral output less that sector's purchases of intermediate input. Substituting the value sum of deliveries to intermediate and final demands, equation (3–19), for the value of total output in (3–9) yields

$$q_j^v V_j = \sum_i p_j X_{ji} + q_j^y Y_j - \sum_i p_i X_{ij} \qquad (j = 11, 2, \ldots, n) \tag{3–29}$$

Summing (3–29) over all sectors produces the expected result:

$$\sum_j q_j^v V_j = \sum_j q_j^y Y_j \tag{3–30}$$

since

$$\sum_j \sum_i p_j X_{ji} = \sum_j \sum_i p_i X_{ij}$$

the value of total deliveries to intermediate demand equals the value of total intermediate input purchases.

Proposition 2 follows directly from (3–28) and (3–30):

$$E_v = E_y \tag{3–31}$$

The different initial descriptions of macroeconomic objectives and microeconomic production offered by value-added and delivery-to-final-demand models are of no consequence to productivity accounting in a closed economy. The models produce identical measures of aggregate productivity growth.

The Open Economy

The derivation of the open economy model parallels the development of its closed economy counterpart. The only important difference is that imported inputs (M_{mj}) enter both the aggregate production-possibilities frontier and the sectoral production functions. Society's production problem is to maximize aggregate deliveries to final demand (μ)

$$\mu = H\ (Y_1, Y_2, \ldots, Y_n, L_{11}, L_{12}, \ldots, L_{rn}, K_{11}, K_{12}, \ldots, K_{sn}, M_{11}, \ldots, M_{un}, t) \tag{3–32}$$

subject to fixed supplies of domestic labor and capital inputs, market equilibrium conditions, and linearly homogeneous sectoral production functions:

$$Z_j = h^j\ (L_{1j}, L_{2j}, \ldots, L_{rj}, K_{1j}, K_{2j}, \ldots, K_{sj}, X_{1j}, X_{2j}, \ldots X_{nj}, M_{1j}, M_{2j}, \ldots, M_{uj}, t) \quad (j = 1, 2, \ldots, n) \tag{3–33}$$

Like the production function g^j defined in (3–14), h^j describes an unconstrained model of sectoral production.[9]

It is important to emphasize that modeling aggregate production and productivity growth has particular implications for the treatment of imports and exports. Imported inputs must appear in both the aggregate and sectoral models of production, equations (3–32) and (3–33), respectively. Imports delivered directly to domestic final demand, however, are not included in either model since, by definition, they do not enter domestic production accounts. In short, imported final products bear no influence on domestic productivity measurement, the subject of this paper. At the same time, all exports are included in the models and considered an element of the domestic economy's deliveries to final demand—that is, exports are goods and services produced domestically but not consumed internally. Note, it is not necessary to decompose these deliveries to final demand into deliveries to domestic and foreign markets. In an aggregate model of a nation's productivity growth, there is no more need to make this distinction than there is to distinguish sectoral output by destination in a sectoral model of productivity growth.[10]

The formal development of an aggregate open-economy model begins then with the production model (3–32). Setting the aggregate value of μ equal to unity, the constant-returns-to-scale function H can be expressed as a production-possibilities frontier:

$$1 = H\,(Y_1, Y_2, \ldots, Y_n, L_{11}, L_{12}, \ldots, L_{rn}, K_{11}, K_{12}, \ldots, K_{sn}, M_{11}, M_{12}, \ldots, M_{un}, t) \tag{3–34}$$

Homogeneity and market equilibrium conditions together imply:

$$\frac{\partial \ln H}{\partial \ln Y_j} = \frac{-q_j^y Y_j}{\sum_j q_j^y Y_j} \qquad (j = 1, 2, \ldots, n)$$

$$\frac{\partial \ln H}{\partial \ln L_{lj}} = \frac{p_{lj} L_{lj}}{\sum_j q_j^y Y_j} \qquad (j = 1, 2, \ldots, n)$$

$$\frac{\partial \ln H}{\partial \ln K_{kj}} = \frac{p_{kj} K_{kj}}{\sum_j q_j^y Y_j} \qquad (j = 1, 2, \ldots, n)$$

$$\frac{\partial \ln H}{\partial \ln M_{mj}} = \frac{p_m M_{mj}}{\sum_j q_j^y Y_j} \qquad (j = 1, 2, \ldots, n) \tag{3–35}$$

and

$$\sum_j \frac{\partial \ln H}{\partial \ln Y_j} = -\sum_j \frac{q_j^y Y_j}{\sum_j q_j^y Y_j} = -1$$

$$\sum_j \sum_l \frac{\partial \ln H}{\partial \ln L_{lj}} + \sum_j \sum_k \frac{\partial \ln H}{\partial \ln K_{kj}} + \sum_j \sum_m \frac{\partial \ln H}{\partial \ln M_{mj}}$$

$$= \sum_j \sum_l \frac{p_{lj} L_{lj}}{\sum_j q_j^y Y_j} + \sum_j \sum_k \frac{P_{kj} K_{kj}}{\sum_j q_j^y Y_j} + \sum_j \sum_m \frac{p_m M_{mj}}{\sum_j q_j^y Y_j} = 1 \tag{3–36}$$

where p_m is the price of the mth imported input.[11]

The rate of aggregate productivity growth (E'_y) appropriate for an open economy is derived by substituting the necessary conditions for producer equilibrium (3–35) into the total time derivative of the aggregate frontier H.

The resulting expression is

$$E'_y \equiv \frac{\partial \ln H}{\partial t} = \sum_j \frac{q_j^y Y_j}{\sum_j q_j^y Y_j} \frac{d \ln Y_j}{dt} - \sum_j \sum_l \frac{p_{lj} L_{lj}}{\sum_j q_j^y Y_j} \frac{d \ln L_{lj}}{dt}$$

$$- \sum_j \sum_k \frac{p_{kj} K_{kj}}{\sum_j q_j^y Y_j} \frac{d \ln K_{kj}}{dt} - \sum_j \sum_m \frac{p_m M_{mj}}{\sum_j q_j^y Y_j} \frac{d \ln M_{mj}}{dt} \quad (3\text{–}37)$$

Comparing the expressions for E_y and E'_y defined in (3–23) and (3–37), respectively, leads to the following proposition:

Proposition 3. The rate of aggregate productivity growth for an economy maximizing aggregate output (deliveries to final demand) is defined as the weighted average of rates of growth of sectoral deliveries to final demand (with weights equal to sectoral delivery-to-final-demand shares in aggregate output) less the weighted average of rates of growth of primary inputs (with weights equal to the value shares of input payments in aggregate output). Both sets of weights sum to unity. For a closed economy, primary inputs include domestic supplies of labor and capital. For an open economy, primary inputs include domestic labor and capital *and* imported materials.

The most important finding of this paper follows from Propositions 1 and 3. It concerns the relation between E_v and E'_y, the measures of aggregate productivity growth respectively derived from value-added and delivery-to-final-demand models for an open economy. The result can be stated as a proposition.

Proposition 4. For an economy *open* to trade in foreign-produced inputs, the rate of aggregate productivity growth derived from a value-added model of aggregate production is *greater* than the corresponding rate resulting from a delivery-to-final-demand model. The two rates differ by an amount that is proportional to the value share of the economy's imported materials in total deliveries to final demand.

Proving this proposition begins with both the sectoral accounting identity (3–19), equating the value of each sector's output to the sum of the values of its deliveries to intermediate and final demands, and the accounting identity defining the value of sectoral value added in an open economy:

$$q_j^v V_j = q_j Z_j - \sum_i p_i X_{ij} - \sum_m p_m M_{mj} \qquad (j = 1, 2, \ldots, n) \quad (3\text{–}38)$$

The total derivative of (3–19) with respect to time is expressed in equation (3–25). The time derivative of (3–38) is

$$\frac{d \ln V_j}{dt} = \frac{q_j Z_j}{q_j^v V_j} \frac{d \ln Z_j}{dt} - \sum_i \frac{p_i X_{ij}}{q_j^v V_j} \frac{d \ln X_{ij}}{dt} - \sum_m \frac{p_m M_{mj}}{q_j^v V_j} \frac{d \ln M_{mj}}{dt} \quad (j = 1, 2, \ldots, n) \qquad (3\text{–}39)$$

Subsituting (3–25) into (3–39) and substituting the resulting expression for the growth of sectoral value added into equation (3–12), the expression for E_v yields

$$E_v = \sum_j \frac{q_j^y Y_j}{\sum_j q_j^v V_j} \frac{d \ln Y_j}{dt} - \sum_j \sum_l \frac{p_{lj} L_{lj}}{\sum_j q_j^v V_j} \frac{d \ln L_{lj}}{dt} - \sum_j \sum_k \frac{p_{kj} K_{kj}}{\sum_j q_j^v V_j} \frac{d \ln K_{kj}}{dt} - \sum_j \sum_m \frac{p_m M_{mj}}{\sum_j q_j^v V_j} \frac{d \ln M_{mj}}{dt} \qquad (3\text{–}40)$$

Multiplying (3–40) by the ratio $\Sigma_j q_j^v V_j / \Sigma_j q_j^y Y_j$ produces an expression equal to the definition of E_y' in (3–37) so that

$$E_v = \frac{\sum_j q_j^y Y_j}{\sum_j q_j^v V_j} E_y' \qquad (3\text{–}41)$$

Equation (3–41) has precisely the same form as equation (3–28), the expression relating the aggregate productivity rates E_v and E_y for an economy closed to imported inputs. The difference is that the ratio $\Sigma q_j^y Y_j / \Sigma q_j^v V_j$ equals unity for a closed economy, as demonstrated above, but is greater than unity for an open economy. Substituting (3–19) for the value of total output, $q_j Z_j$, in (3–38) and summing over all n sectors yields

$$\sum_j q_j^v V_j = \sum_j q_j^y Y_j - \sum_j \sum_m p_m M_{mj} \qquad (3\text{–}42)$$

The value of aggregate deliveries to final demand (aggregate output) exceeds the value of aggregate value added (net output) by an amount equal to the value of imported inputs.

Proposition 4 follows directly. Substituting (3–42) into (3–41) yields

$$E_v = \left[\frac{\sum_j q_j^y Y_j}{\sum_j q_j^y Y_j - \sum_j \sum_m p_m M_{mj}} \right] E_y' \qquad (3\text{–}43)$$

It necessarily follows that $E_v > E'_y$ and, verifying proposition 4,

$$E'_y = \left(1 - \frac{\sum_j \sum_m p_m M_{mj}}{\sum_j q^y_j Y_j}\right) E_v \qquad (3\text{–}44)$$

the two rates differ by an amount that is proportional to the value share of the economy's imported materials in total deliveries to final demand. Value-added and delivery-to-final-demand models of aggregate production produce identical measures of aggregate productivity growth if and only if the economy is closed to trade in foreign-produced inputs ($\Sigma_m p_m M_{mj} = 0$).

3.4. Aggregation over Sectors in an Open Economy

The value-added and delivery-to-final-demand models of aggregate production are each constrained by different microeconomic models of production. These micro models describe sectoral productivity growth which, in turn, determines aggregate productivity growth. The objective of this section is to derive the economic relation between sectoral and aggregate meaures of productivity growth for an economy open to trade in foreign-produced inputs. The value-added and delivery-to-final-demand models are contrasted.

Sectoral Productivity Growth

The value-added separable production functions f^j defined in (3–4) describe microeconomic production in the aggregate value-added model. Given value-added separability, the subfunctions V^j defined in (3–2) become the effective constraints for the aggregate value-added maximization problem (3–1). These functions contain all the important properties describing sectoral productivity growth. Expressing the logarithmic derivative of V^j with respect to time in terms of sectoral conditions for producer equilibrium results in an expression that can be solved for the measured rate of sectoral productivity growth (e^j_v):[12]

$$e^j_v \equiv \frac{\partial \ln V^j}{\partial t} = \frac{d \ln V_j}{dt} - \sum_l \frac{p_{lj} L_{lj}}{q^v_j V_j} \frac{d \ln L_{lj}}{dt} - \sum_k \frac{p_{kj} K_{kj}}{q^v_j V_j} \frac{d \ln K_{kj}}{dt} \qquad (j = 1, 2, \ldots, n) \qquad (3\text{–}45)$$

Neither foreign-produced inputs nor domestically produced intermediate inputs enter this description of sectoral productivity growth.

Microeconomic production in the delivery-to-final-demand model is characterized by the sectoral production functions h^j defined in (3–33). They constrain the aggregate production problem (3–32) directly. The measured rate of sectoral productivity growth (e_z^j) can be solved[13] from the logarithmic time derivative of (3–33) with conditions for producer equilibrium imposed:[14]

$$e_z^j \equiv \frac{\partial \ln h^j}{\partial t} = \frac{d \ln Z_j}{dt} - \sum_l \frac{p_{lj} L_{lj}}{q_j Z_j} \frac{d \ln L_{lj}}{dt} - \sum_k \frac{p_{kj} K_{kj}}{q_j Z_j} \frac{d \ln K_{kj}}{dt}$$

$$- \sum_i \frac{p_i X_{ij}}{q_j Z_j} \frac{d \ln X_{ij}}{dt} - \sum_m \frac{p_m M_{mj}}{q_j Z_j} \frac{d \ln M_{mj}}{dt} \quad (j = 1, 2, \ldots, n) \qquad (3\text{–}46)$$

The rates of sectoral productivity growth depend on both intersectoral and international transactions.

It is important to emphasize that the variables e_v^j and e_z^j describe different rates of sectoral productivity growth. The following proposition holds for an "open" economy.

> *Proposition 5.* For an economy open to trade in foreign-produced inputs, the rate of sectoral productivity growth derived from a sectoral net output (value added) production function is *greater* than the corresponding rate resulting from a sectoral gross output production function. The two rates differ by an amount that is proportional to the share of the sector's purchases of domestic intermediate and foreign-produced inputs in the value of sectoral gross output.

Formally demonstrating this proposition begins with substituting equation (3–39), the logarithmic time derivative of value added, into equation (3–45) defining e_v^j:

$$e_v^j = \left(\frac{q_j Z_j}{q_j^v V_j} \frac{d \ln Z_j}{dt} - \sum_i \frac{p_i X_{ij}}{q_j^v V_j} \frac{d \ln X_{ij}}{dt} - \sum_m \frac{p_m M_{mj}}{q_j^v V_j} \frac{d \ln M_{mj}}{dt} \right)$$

$$- \sum_l \frac{p_{lj} L_{lj}}{q_j^v V_j} \frac{d \ln L_{lj}}{dt} - \sum_k \frac{p_{kj} K_{kj}}{q_j^v V_j} \frac{d \ln K_{kj}}{dt} \quad (j = 1, 2, \ldots, n) \qquad (3\text{–}47)$$

Substituting (3–46) into (3–47) yields

$$e_v^j = \left(\frac{q_j Z_j}{q_j Z_j - \sum_i p_i X_{ij} - \sum_m p_m M_{mj}}\right) e_z^j \qquad (j = 1, 2, \ldots, n) \quad (3\text{–}48)$$

It necessarily follows that $e_v^j > e_z^j$ and

$$e_z^j = \left(1 - \frac{\sum_i p_i X_{ij} + \sum_m p_m M_{mj}}{q_j Z_j}\right) e_v^j \qquad (j = 1, 2, \ldots, n) \quad (3\text{–}49)$$

the two rates differ by an amount that is proportional to the share of sectoral purchases of domestically produced and foreign-produced inputs in the value of sectoral gross output.[15]

Aggregation

This paper has emphasized the fundamentally different characterizations of economic activity offered by value-added and delivery-to-final-demand models of economic growth. These differences are nowhere more apparent than in the formulas defining E_y' and E_v as aggregate rates of productivity growth formed from the sectoral measures e_z^j and e_v^j, respectively. Since e_z^j is generated from a sectoral model incorporating interindustry and international transactions, the aggregating algorithm must capture the contributions of each sector's productivity growth through deliveries of its output to both final *and* intermediate demand. In contrast, since the sectoral model maintaining value-added separability abstracts from all intersectoral and international transactions, aggregating over e_v^j must capture sectoral advances in productivity transmitted only through value-added contributions to aggregate net output.

Both aggregate and sectoral value-added models view the economy as a set of horizontally independent sectors. The relevant measure of sectoral output is the quantity of value added. The aggregate economy's production-possibilities frontier is defined in terms of the sectoral quantities of value added. Both models consider only labor and capital inputs. The formal link between the aggregate and sectoral rates E_v and e_v^j is simple and direct.

Proposition 6. The rate of aggregate productivity growth E_v for a value-added model of aggregate production equals a weighted *average* of the sectoral rates of productivity growth e_v^j, with weights equal to sectoral value shares of value added in total value added.

This result is derived by substituting the expression for e^j_v, equation (3–45), into equation (3–12), the expression for E_v:

$$E_v = \sum_j \frac{q^v_j V_j}{\sum_j q^v_j V_j} e^j_v \tag{3–50}$$

The delivery-to-final-demand model of aggregate production and its microeconomic production constraints view the economy as consisting of vertically interrelated sectors depending not only on each other but on international trade as well. Aggregate and sectoral models each define output in terms of *its* particular final product. While deliveries to final demand define output at the aggregate level, individual sectors produce output delivered to both final and intermediate demands. Similarly, each model considers all inputs primary to *its* particular production process. The economy's primary inputs include labor, capital, and imported inputs. Sectors employ labor, capital, imported inputs, and domestically produced intermediate inputs. Given this vertical model of economic activity, advances in productivity in an individual industry contribute to aggregate economic growth both directly through deliveries to final demand and indirectly through increased deliveries to sectors dependent on its output as intermediate input. The aggregation formula must capture both direct and indirect transmissions of sectoral productivity growth.

Proposition 7. The rate of aggregate productivity growth E'_y for a delivery-to-final-demand model of aggregate production equals a weighted *sum* of the sectoral rates of productivity growth e^j_z, with weights equal to sectoral ratios of the value of gross output to the value of total deliveries to final demand.

Demonstrating this proposition begins with equation (3–19), the expression equating the value of each sector's total output to the sum of the values of intermediate demand for that output by all n sectors and the value of final demand for that output. Substituting the logarithmic derivative of (3–19) with respect to time, equation (3–25), into (3–46) permits the measure of sectoral productivity to be expressed in terms identifying the immediate uses of the sector's output:

$$e^j_z = \sum_i \frac{p_j X_{ji}}{q_j Z_j} \frac{d \ln X_{ji}}{dt} + \frac{q^y_j Y_j}{q_j Z_j} \frac{d \ln Y_j}{dt} - \sum_l \frac{p_{lj} L_{lj}}{q_j Z_j} \frac{d \ln L_{lj}}{dt}$$

$$- \sum_k \frac{p_{kj} K_{kj}}{q_j Z_j} \frac{d \ln K_{kj}}{dt} - \sum_i \frac{p_i X_{ij}}{q_j Z_j} \frac{d \ln X_{ij}}{dt} - \sum_m \frac{p_m M_{mj}}{q_j Z_j} \frac{d \ln M_{mj}}{dt}$$

$$(j = 1, 2, \ldots, n) \tag{3–51}$$

Multiplying (3–51) by the ratio $q_j Z_j / \Sigma q_j^y Y_j$ and summing over all n sectors produces the economic relation between sectoral and aggregate measures of productivity growth:

$$E_y' = \sum_j \frac{q_j Z_j}{\sum_j q_j^y Y_j} e_z^j \tag{3–52}$$

The sum of the weights in (3–52) exceeds unity by an amount equal to the ratio of the aggregate value of deliveries to intermediate demand to the aggregate value of deliveries to final demand:

$$\sum_j \frac{q_j Z_j}{\sum_j q_j^y Y_j} = \sum_j \left(\frac{\sum_i p_j X_{ji} + q_j^y Y_j}{\sum_j q_j^y Y_j} \right) = \sum_j \frac{\sum_i p_j X_{ji}}{\sum_j q_j^y Y_j} + 1 \tag{3–53}$$

The weights sum to a value larger than unity because each sector contributes to the rate of productivity growth for the aggregate economy through its deliveries to both final and intermediate demand. Gollop (1979) presents an heuristic interpretation of this weighting structure:

> Consider an individual sector that experiences an advance in its rate of technical change. Holding constant all primary and intermediate inputs, the sector can provide the economy with increased output. The objective of creating the appropriate weight for this sector's technological advance is to correctly assign causal responsibility to this sector for any effect on aggregate technical change. Since the ultimate macroeconomic concern is the effect of this technical change on aggregate output, the appropriate denominator in the weight is the sum of all n sector contributions to aggregate output. Since the individual sector transmits the benefits of its productivity growth to final consumers both directly through deliveries to final demand and indirectly through deliveries to intermediate demand, the appropriate numerator in the weight is the sector's total output, i.e., the sum of its deliveries to final and intermediate demand.[16]

Gollop (1979) concludes that the appropriately weighted sum contributions of sectoral productivity growth to aggregate productivity growth are identical whether the sectoral rates are derived from gross-output or value-added models of sectoral production. This implies

$$\sum_j \frac{q_j Z_j}{\sum_j q_j^y Y_j} e_z^j = \sum_j \frac{q_j^v V_j}{\sum_j q_j^v V_j} e_v^j \tag{3–54}$$

It is important to recognize that this result holds only for a closed economy. Given (3–50) and (3–52), proposition 4 suggests

$$\sum_j \frac{q_j Z_j}{\sum_j q_j^y Y_j} e_z^j = E_y' = \left(1 - \frac{\sum_j \sum_m p_m M_{mj}}{\sum_j q_j^y Y_j}\right) E_v$$

$$= \left(1 - \frac{\sum_j \sum_m p_m M_{mj}}{\sum_j q_j^y Y_j}\right) \sum_j \frac{q_j^v V_j}{\sum_j q_j^v V_j} e_v^j \qquad (3\text{–}55)$$

Equation (3–54) holds *if and only if*

$$\sum_j \sum_m p_m M_{mj} = 0$$

the economy is closed to trade in foreign-produced inputs.

Conclusion

Value-added and delivery-to-final-demand models of aggregate production offer fundamentally different descriptions of macroeconomic and microeconomic activity. For an economy open to trade in foreign-produced inputs, those differences have important implications for the measured rate of aggregate productivity growth. This paper demonstrates that the two models produce measures that differ in direct proportion to the extent of the economy's dependence on imported inputs. The important remaining question is: Which model forms a more appropriate basis for measuring aggregate productivity growth?

The answer follows directly from the arguments developed throughout this paper. First, productivity growth is a measure of economic performance. Performance measures should serve as barometers, sensitive to the economy's success in solving its economic problem. The choice of productivity measure therefore depends on society's objectives. Economists long have recognized that society's economic objective is to satisfy human wants through deliveries to final demand.[17] Second, the solution to society's economic problem is constrained by scarce resources. Productivity growth measures how well the economy allocates its scarce resources among its producing agents. Primary inputs for the macro economy include labor, capital, and imported inputs. These plus domestically produced intermediate inputs form the primary inputs for each micro sector. Productivity growth views all primary inputs symmetrically. Unless affirmed by economic evidence, value-added separability is an inappropriate as well as unnecessary assumption. Third, the economy does not consist of horizontally independent sectors. It is, instead, a set of vertically interdependent sectors dependent on both intersectoral and international transactions. Only the delivery-to-final-demand model recognizes these transactions. Only it describes how an individual sector transmits the benefits of its productivity growth to final consumers both directly through deliveries to final demand and indirectly through deliveries to intermediate demand. Fourth, a measure of aggregate productivity growth is useful only as a comparative measure of economic performance over time or across countries. Only the delivery-to-final-demand model is sensitive to the intertemporal and international variation in imported input requirements.

Accepting or rejecting these arguments and their implicit conclusion is much more than an academic exercise. It has important practical consequences for both intertemporal and international comparisons of productivity growth. Table 3–1 reports the current price ratios of imported inputs to deliveries to final demand for selected years for eight industrial nations. Not surprisingly, most of the ratios not only increase over time and increase at different rates but also vary considerably across countries. It follows from equation (3–44) that the rates E_v *and* E'_y maintain no constant relation either across countries or over time.

The practical implications for intertemporal productivity comparisons

Table 3–1. Current Price Ratios of Imported Inputs to Deliveries-to-Final-Demand[a]

	1950[b]	*1953*	*1957*	*1960*	*1966*	*1969*	*1973*	*1977*[c]
Canada	0.196	0.187	0.198	0.184	0.202	0.184	0.186	0.194
France	0.140	0.136	0.139	0.132	0.131	0.136	0.153	0.181
Germany	0.109	0.115	0.159	0.151	0.162	0.151	0.147	0.181
Italy	0.119	0.116	0.128	0.135	0.138	0.148	0.181	0.222
Japan	0.114	0.118	0.131	0.107	0.101	0.093	0.097	0.121
Netherlands	0.326	0.303	0.329	0.318	0.308	0.296	0.300	0.311
United Kingdom	0.185	0.184	0.178	0.178	0.160	0.174	0.195	0.229
United States	0.036	0.033	0.035	0.034	0.037	0.040	0.053	0.081

[a]Current price imported inputs are defined as the product of gross imports reported in OECD (1970, 1979) and the ratio of imported inputs to total imports calculated from data reported in U.N. Department of International Economic and Trade Affairs (1978). Deliveries to final demand equal the sum of national income (including subsidies but excluding indirect business taxes) and imported inputs. All data are stated in national currencies.

[b]The ratios for Italy and Japan refer to 1951 and 1952, respectively.

[c]The ratio for Japan refers to 1976.

follow directly from the trends observed in Table 3–1. The U.S. ratio doubled between 1969 and 1977. During the same period, the ratios for Italy and France increased by 50% and 33% respectively, while the ratio increased by only 5% in the Netherlands. If one accepts the premise that aggregate economic growth should be evaluated in a delivery-to-final-demand framework, then one concludes that the value-added model produces not only an upward biased but also an increasingly upward biased measure of postwar aggregate economic performance. The extent of the intertemporal bias depends on the change over time in a nation's dependence on imported inputs.[18]

The consequences for international productivity comparisons are equally important. Table 3–2 reports both rates of aggregate productivity growth for the eight nations. As expected, the differential is small for the United States while large for most other nations—most notably, the Netherlands. Conclusions regarding relative productivity growth across nations may be biased by a value-added model, especially comparisons involving nations with very different imported input requirements.

The summary conclusion of this paper is that the delivery-to-final-demand model provides the appropriate framework in which to measure and analyze aggregate productivity performance. It produces measures that offer the most meaningful intertemporal and international productivity comparisons. Looking to future research, only it offers a framework for evaluating regional productivity growth among trading nations.[19] Stated alternatively, just as *intersectoral* transactions are an important component of sectoral models of

Table 3–2. Average Annual Growth Rates of Aggregate Productivity Growth: 1957–1973

	Value-Added Model[a] E_v	*Delivery-to-Final-Demand Model* E'_y
Canada	0.0158	0.0127
France	0.0306	0.0261
Germany	0.0308	0.0260
Italy	0.0326	0.0275
Japan	0.0410	0.0363
Netherlands	0.0233	0.0159
United Kingdom	0.0199	0.0162
United States	0.0123	0.0117

[a]The average annual growth rates reported for the value-added model are calculated from the growth rates reported in Christensen, Cummings, and Jorgenson (1980), Table 11.10.

productivity growth, so too *international* transactions are an important component in an aggregate model of productivity growth. Excluding trade at the aggregate level is analogous to excluding intermediate input at the sectoral level.

Notes

1. Kendrick (1973), p. 16.
2. *Ibid.*
3. This condition will be demonstrated formally in section 3.2.
4. Deliveries to final demand include conventional goods and services as well as less tangible but no less important products like health, safety, and environmental quality.
5. For a detailed discussion of value-added separability, see Gollop (1979), pp. 320–22.
6. Note that the intermediate input prices p_i do not have j subscripts. It is assumed that there is no price discrimination across sectors in the market for intermediate inputs. All sectors pay the same f.o.b. price for the same intermediate input.
7. Note that there is no requirement that the price of the jth sector's deliveries to final demand equal the price of that sector's deliveries to intermediate demand.
8. This result will be stated formally as part of Proposition 3 below.
9. Note that domestically produced intermediate inputs enter the problem through the production constraints (3–33). At the economy-wide level, however, all sales and purchases of domestically produced intermediate inputs are offsetting transactions.
10. An economic model of *regional* productivity growth would distinguish deliveries to domestic and foreign markets. Furthermore, each nation's exports to final and intermediate demands would be distinguished.
11. The fact that the input shares in aggregate output sum to unity can be verified from the sectoral accounting identity:

$$\sum_i p_j X_{ji} + q_j^y Y_j = \sum_l p_{lj} L_{lj} + \sum_k p_{kj} K_{kj} + \sum_i p_i X_{ij} + \sum_m p_m M_{mj}$$

Summing the identity over all n sectors produces the result required by (3–36):

$$\sum_j q_j^y Y_j = \sum_j \sum_l p_{lj} L_{lj} + \sum_j \sum_k p_{kj} K_{kj} + \sum_j \sum_m p_m M_{mj}$$

Note that import prices p_m do not have j subscripts. It is assumed that all domestic sectors pay the same f.o.b. price for identical imported materials.

12. Competitive equilibrium conditions at the sectoral level require that output elasticities with respect to inputs equal the corresponding value shares of input payments in sectoral output:

$$\frac{\partial \ln L_{lj}}{\partial t} = \frac{p_{lj} L_{lj}}{q_j^v V_j} \qquad (l = 1, 2, \ldots, r;\ j = 1, 2, \ldots, n)$$

$$\frac{\partial \ln K_{kj}}{\partial t} = \frac{p_{kj} K_{kj}}{q_j^v V_j} \qquad (k = 1, 2, \ldots, s;\ j = 1, 2, \ldots, n)$$

Since the function V^j exhibits constant returns to scale, the output elasticities and the value shares both sum to unity.

13. Note that the variable defining the sectoral rate of productivity growth is subscripted with z, not y. Subject to production and market constraints, sectoral producers maximize gross output Z_j, not deliveries to final demand Y_j.

14. Market conditions for producer equilibrium require:

$$\frac{\partial \ln L_{lj}}{\partial t} = \frac{p_{lj}L_{lj}}{q_j Z_j} \qquad (l = 1, 2, \ldots, r;\ j = 1, 2, \ldots, n)$$

$$\frac{\partial \ln K_{kj}}{\partial t} = \frac{p_{kj}K_{kj}}{q_j Z_j} \qquad (k = 1, 2, \ldots, s;\ j = 1, 2, \ldots, n)$$

$$\frac{\partial \ln X_{ij}}{\partial t} = \frac{p_i X_{ij}}{q_j Z_j} \qquad (i = 1, 2, \ldots, n;\ j = 1, 2, \ldots, n)$$

$$\frac{\partial \ln M_{mj}}{\partial t} = \frac{p_m M_{mj}}{q_j Z_j} \qquad (m = 1, 2, \ldots, u;\ j = 1, 2, \ldots, n)$$

Linear homogeneity requires that both the output elasticities and the value shares each sum to unity.

15. Note that even if the jth sector imports no foreign-produced inputs ($\Sigma_m p_m M_{mj} = 0$), the measure e^j_v is still greater than e^j_z. The relation between e^j_v and e^j_z in a "closed" economy is discussed in Gollop (1979).

16. Gollop (1979), pp. 330–331.

17. See note 4.

18. The increasing U.S. dependence on imported inputs is neither restricted to a few producing sectors nor is it limited to the post-1973 era. Gollop and Roberts (1981) study the importance of imported inputs to 21 two-digit manufacturing industries over the 1948–1973 period. They find that the cost share of imported materials in total production cost increased in 17 of 21 sectors. More importantly, they find that this shift in cost shares is the result of real input usage, not simple price effects. The average annual rate of growth in real imported materials across all manufacturing industries is 6.7%. The average among durable goods industries is 8.8%. The rate of growth in imported input exceeds the growth rate for capital and labor inputs and even domestic materials in 16 of 21 manufacturing sectors.

19. A well-designed model of regional productivity would examine how efficiently the regional economy uses inputs under it control to produce output for regional final demand and foreign markets. The model would consider not only labor, capital, and nationally produced and consumed intermediate inputs but also all intraregional imports and exports and all regional imports of foreign-produced material inputs.

References

Christensen, L. R., and D. W. Jorgenson, 1973, "Measuring the Performance of the Private Sector of the U.S. Economy, 1929–1969," in M. Moss, ed., *Measuring Economic and Social Performance* (New York: National Bureau of Economic Research), pp. 233–338.

Christensen, L. R.; Dianne Cummings; and Dale W. Jorgenson, 1980, "Economic Growth, 1947–73: An International Comparison," in J. W. Kendrick and B. N. Vaccara, eds., *New Developments in Productivity Measurement and Analysis* (Chicago: University of Chicago Press for the NBER).

Denison, E. F., 1962, *Sources of Economic Growth in the United States and the Alternatives Before Us* (New York: Committee for Economic Development).

Denison, E. F., 1974, *Accounting for United States Economic Growth, 1929–1969* (Washington, D.C.: Brookings Institution).

Denison, E. F., 1979, *Accounting for Slower Economic Growth: The United States in the 1970s* (Washington, D.C.: Brookings Institution).

Gollop, F. M., 1979, "Accounting for Intermediate Input: The Link Between Sectoral and Aggregate Measures of Productivity Growth," in A. Rees and J. Kendrick, eds., *The Measurement and Interpretation of Productivity* (Washington, D.C.: National Academy of Sciences).

Gollop, F. M., and M. J. R., 1981, "Imported Intermediate Input: Impact on Sectoral Productivity in U.S. Manufacturing," in A. Dogramaci and N. Adam, eds., *Aggregate and Industry Level Productivity Analysis* (Boston: Martinus Nijhoff).

Jorgenson, D. W., and Z. Griliches, 1967, "The Explanation of Productivity Change," *Review of Economic Studies,* 34:249–283.

Kendrick, J. W., 1961, *Productivity Trends in the United States,* National Bureau of Economic Research (Princeton: Princeton University Press).

Kendrick, J. W., 1973, *Postwar Productivity Trends in the United States, 1948–1969* (New York: National Bureau of Economic Research).

Kendrick, J. W., and E. S. Grossman, 1980, *Productivity in the United States: Trends and Cycles* (Baltimore and London: The Johns Hopkins University Press).

Organization for Economic Cooperation and Development, 1970, *National Accounts of OECD Countries, 1950–1968* (Paris: OECD).

Organization for Economic Cooperation and Development, 1979, *National Accounts of OECD Countries, 1952–1977* (Paris: OECD).

Solow, R. M., 1957, "Technical Change and the Aggregate Production Function," *Review of Economics and Statistics* 39 (3):312–320.

United Nations Department of International Economic and Social Affairs, 1978, *Yearbook of International Trade Statistics 1977* (New York: United Nations).

4 A COMPARISON OF ALTERNATIVE FRONTIER-COST FUNCTION SPECIFICATIONS

T. Cowing, D. Reifschneider, and R. Stevenson

4.1. Introduction

Most economic relationships are based upon optimization of an objective, e.g., the maximization of welfare or the minimization of costs. Optimization involves a search for maximum or minimum values subject only to the barriers of binding constraints. The locus of constrained maximum or minimum values defines a *frontier*, a set of best obtainable positions. In the case of the firm, a production function frontier identifies maximum obtainable outputs given available factor inputs and existing production technologies; a cost function frontier identifies minimum obtainable costs given output levels, factor input prices, and existing production technologies; and a profit function frontier identifies maximum obtainable profit levels given output prices (and associated demand relationships), factor input prices, and existing production technologies.

The failure to attain a position on the frontier signifies inefficiency with respect to the stated objective and specified constraints. Inefficient performance may reflect a conflict of objectives among participants (Leibenstein, 1966); a misspecification of objectives (Stigler, 1976); a failure to identify all relevant binding constraints (e.g., Averch and Johnson, 1962); or simple ineptitude. Regardless of the source of inefficiency, in any given setting it is unlikely that all (or possibly any) observations will lie on the frontier of normative or positive interest.

Traditional econometric techniques may not be suitable to estimating frontier relationships. For example, a cost function estimated by least squares is essentially a reflection of the average performance of firms in the industry. Deviations from the estimated function sum to zero since one statistically expects the firm's costs to lie on the estimated cost curve. But the true cost function, the frontier function, is the relationship between minimum levels of cost on one hand, and given sets of input prices and output levels on the other. Deviations due to inefficiency from the frontier cost curve should be in one direction only, the direction of increased cost. Thus estimation of a cost function by least squares should produce an average performance cost function that lies above the true frontier.

However, the assumption that all observed deviations from the frontier can only take place in one direction may be too strict. Though deviations due to inefficiency can only take on positive values for costs or negative values for production, the concept of a frontier function can encompass stochastic elements. Production processes may have random components unrelated to inefficiency, e.g., weather conditions and machinery performance, or random components due to measurement error in the dependent variable. While it is possible to argue that a true frontier exists only under conditions of perfect weather and machine performance, it is perhaps preferable to allow for a normal symmetric random component for the frontier function. It is not necessary to restrict frontiers to be solely deterministic.[1]

Substantial progress has been made in recent years in developing statistically acceptable frontier estimators. Aigner, Amemiya, and Poirier (1976), Aigner, Lovell and Schmidt (1977), and Meussen and van den Broeck (1977) have constructed explicit models of the error disturbance that allow for both random error about the frontier—the stochastic element of the frontier—and for one-sided error—the inefficiency effect. With these models, the authors are able to estimate the parameters of the frontier function by maximum likelihood techniques. Greene (1980) has also developed a deterministic frontier model suitable for maximum likelihood estimation. As Greene demonstrates, one-sided inefficiency error distributed as gamma meets the maximum likelihood regulatory conditions. These efforts, however, are subject to the potential criticism that the shape or position of the estimated frontier may be effected by the choice of the assumed distribution of the inefficiency error.

The goal of this study is to compare the effect of various inefficiency error specifications on the estimates of the frontier function parameters. In the following sections we assume that the frontier error disturbance is either one-sided (distributed as GAMMA), or the error has two components: a stochastic component which is normally distributed, and an inefficiency component distributed either exponentially or truncated normally. Using maximum likelihood techniques, estimates of a cost frontier are obtained. The frontier results are compared to a cost function estimated by OLS. The estimates are compared to first determine whether the frontier estimates are *statistically* different from the OLS estimates. As will be shown in the next section, it is possible for all the frontier error models to collapse to the normal distribution, given restrictions on certain parameters. Thus it may be the case that frontier estimation produces results that are statistically indistinguishable from those of the traditional least-squares method.

Even if there are statistical differences between frontier and OLS estimated cost functions, it may be the case that these differences occur only as intercept differences. If this is true then the effect of inefficiency is to neutrally shift the minimum cost function down, leaving price and scale elasticities uneffected. This type of estimated cost curve difference, while important as a measure of firm inefficiency, does not impart any extra information on the relationship of minimum cost to changing economic constraints.

The second consideration for comparison is whether or not OLS and the different frontier specifications produce cost function estimates that are *economically* different. Even if the frontier estimates are statistically different from the OLS estimates, it may be the case that such differences are of little economic importance. This question is of interest, for as will soon be made clear, frontier estimation is considerably more difficult than least squares.

4.2. The Frontier Cost Function

The cost function used in this study is assumed to have the following translog specification:

$$\ln\frac{C_i}{P_{K,i}} = \beta_1 + \beta_2 \ln\frac{P_{F,i}}{P_{K,i}} + \frac{1}{2}\beta_3\left(\ln\frac{P_{Fi}}{P_{Ki}}\right)^2 + \beta_4 \ln\frac{P_{L,i}}{P_{K,i}}$$

$$+\frac{1}{2}\beta_5\left(\ln\frac{P_{Li}}{P_{Ki}}\right)^2 + \beta_6 \ln\frac{P_{F,i}}{P_{K,i}}\ln\frac{P_{L,i}}{P_{K,i}} + \beta_7 \ln Q_i$$

$$+\frac{1}{2}\beta_8(\ln Q_i)^2+\beta_9 \ln Q_i \ln\frac{P_{F,i}}{P_{K,i}}+\beta_{10}\ln Q_i \ln\frac{P_{L,i}}{P_{K,i}}+\varepsilon_i \tag{4-1}$$

where C_i is the total cost of the ith firm; $P_{F,i}$, $P_{L,i}$, and $P_{K,i}$ are prices of fuel, labor, and capital, respectively, for the ith firm; Q_i is the net generation of the ith firm; and ε_i is a disturbance term. Note that homogeneity in prices has been imposed. The error term, ε_i, is assumed to be distributed in a manner consistent with the frontier concept. We consider three alternative distributions for ε_i. The first and second alternative distributions assume that ε_i has a two-component error structure, i.e., $\varepsilon_i = u_i + v_i$. In both cases, v_i is assumed to be normally distributed (v_i represents the stochastic element of the frontier). The error component u_i, on the other hand, represents the inefficiency component of observed cost, and is assumed to be either distributed truncated-normally with zero mode (denoted ALS-TN), or exponentially (denoted ALS-EXP):

$$\text{ALS-TN:}\quad f(u_i\,|\,\sigma_u^2) = [2\pi\sigma_u^2]^{-\frac{1}{2}}\exp\left[-\frac{1}{2}\left(\frac{u_i}{\sigma_u}\right)^2\right] \qquad u_i > 0$$
$$= 0 \qquad u_i \le 0 \tag{4-2}$$

$$\text{ALS-EXP:}\quad f(u_i\,|\,\alpha) = \alpha e^{-\alpha u_i} \qquad u_i > 0$$
$$= 0 \qquad u_i \le 0. \tag{4-3}$$

Given that u_i and v_i are independent, the joint density functions of $\varepsilon_i = v_i + u_i$ are[2]

$$\text{ALS-TN:}\quad f(\varepsilon_i\,|\,\sigma^2, \lambda) = \frac{2}{\sigma} f^*\left(\frac{\varepsilon_i}{\sigma}\right)\left[1 - F^*\left(\frac{-\varepsilon_i\lambda}{\sigma}\right)\right] \tag{4-4}$$

$$\text{ALS-EXP:}\quad f(\varepsilon_i\,|\,\sigma_v^2, \alpha) = \alpha\left[1 - F^*\left(\alpha\sigma_v - \frac{\varepsilon_i}{\sigma_v}\right)\right]\exp\left[\frac{\sigma_v^2\alpha^2}{2} - \alpha\varepsilon_i\right] \tag{4-5}$$

where σ_v^2 is the variance of v_i; $\sigma^2 = \sigma_v^2 + \sigma_u^2$; $\lambda = \sigma_u/\sigma_v$; and f^* and F^* are the standard normal and standard normal cumulative density functions, respectively. The third alternative distribution is the completely one-sided error where ε_i's p.d.f. is the gamma distribution:

$$\text{GAMMA:}\quad f(\varepsilon_i \mid \rho, \gamma) = \frac{\gamma^\rho}{\Gamma(P)}\, \varepsilon_i^{\rho-1}\, e^{-\gamma\varepsilon_i} \qquad \varepsilon_i \geq 0$$

$$= 0 \qquad\qquad \varepsilon < 0 \qquad\qquad (4\text{–}6)$$

where Γ is the gamma operator, $\gamma > 0$, and $\rho > 2$.

Because the mean and variance of ε_i will be useful later on in the paper, we present them here:

	Mean	*Variance*
ALS-TN:	$\sqrt{2/\pi}\,\sigma_u$	$\sigma_u^2[(\pi-2)/\pi] + \sigma_v^2$
ALS-EXP:	$1/\alpha$	$1/\alpha^2 + \sigma_v^2$
GAMMA:	ρ/γ	ρ/γ^2

As inefficiency becomes insignificantly small, the frontier p.d.f.'s become indistinguishable from the normal. The absence of inefficiency may be inferred as $\rho \to \infty$ for GAMMA, $\lambda \to 0$ for ALS-TN, and $\alpha \to \infty$ for ALS-EXP. For GAMMA, as ρ goes to infinity, the gamma distribution becomes more and more symmetric; in the limit, GAMMA's efficiency gain through smaller standard errors vanishes relative to least squares. As Greene (1980) shows, GAMMA estimates become OLS estimates as $(\rho - 2)/\rho \to 1$, ignoring the intercept. However, if ρ is small GAMMA possesses an efficiency advantage over OLS. For the other two distributions, as the inefficiency component approaches zero, the frontier estimator collapses to OLS.

Given the p.d.f.'s of ε_i, the log-likelihood functions of the observed random variable, $\ln C_i/\rho_{K,i}$ may be specified as[2]

$$\text{ALS-TN:}\quad \ln L\left(\ln\frac{C_i}{P_{k,i}} \mid \underline{\beta}, \sigma^2, \lambda\right) = \frac{n}{2}\ln\frac{2}{\pi} - n\ln\sigma - \frac{\Sigma e_i^2}{2\sigma^2}$$

$$+ \sum_1^n \left[\ln\left(1 - F^*\left(-\frac{\varepsilon_i\lambda}{\sigma}\right)\right)\right] \qquad (4\text{–}7)$$

$$\text{ALS-EXP:}\quad \ln L\left(\ln\frac{C_i}{P_{K,i}} \mid \underline{\beta}, \sigma^2, \lambda\right) = n\ln\alpha + \frac{n\,\sigma_v^2\alpha^2}{2} - \alpha\sum_1^n \varepsilon_i$$

$$+\sum_{1}^{n} \ln\left[1 - F^*\left(\alpha\sigma_v - \frac{\varepsilon_i}{\sigma_v}\right)\right] \quad (4\text{–}8)$$

$$\text{GAMMA:} \quad \ln L\left(\ln\frac{C_i}{P_{K,i}} \mid \underline{\beta}, \rho, \gamma\right)$$

$$= n\,\rho\,\ln\gamma - n\,\ln\Gamma(\rho) + (\rho - 1)\sum_{1}^{n}\ln\varepsilon_i - \gamma\sum_{1}^{n}\varepsilon_i \quad (4\text{–}9)$$

where $\varepsilon_i = \ln(C_i/P_{K,i}) - \underline{X}_i'\underline{\beta}$, and $\underline{X}_i$ is defined as in (4–1).

Equations (4–7), (4–8), and (4–9) only use the information present in the cost function. Additional information exists in the cost-share equation. From Shepard's lemma, the share of each input equals the derivative of $\ln(C_i/P_{K,i})$ with respect to the logarithm of its own price (relative to $P_{K,i}$), plus a disturbance term:

$$S_{F,i} = \beta_2 + \beta_3 \ln\frac{P_{F,i}}{P_{K,i}} + \beta_6 \ln\frac{P_{L,i}}{P_{K,i}} + \beta_9 \ln Q_i + \varepsilon_{F,i} \quad (4\text{–}10)$$

$$S_{L,i} = \beta_4 + \beta_5 \ln\frac{P_{L,i}}{P_{K,i}} + \beta_6 \ln\frac{P_{F,i}}{P_{K,i}} + \beta_{10} \ln Q_i + \varepsilon_{L,i} \quad (4\text{–}11)$$

If we could start with the production function and solve for the translog cost function, introducing disturbance terms at appropriate places, e.g., in the production and factor demand equations, we could determine the specific relationship between ε_i and the disturbances of the share equations as Schmidt and Lovell (1979) did for a Cobb-Douglas production function. Unfortunately, this procedure is not feasible in the case of the translog cost function.

As an alternative we make the convenient though somewhat unsatisfactory assumption that the share equation disturbances are multinormally distributed and independent of ε_i. This assumption is valid if there is no allocative inefficiency; with technical inefficiency alone the share equation disturbances are independent of the cost function disturbances. (This assumption is similar to one made by Schmidt and Lovell in the first part of their 1979 paper on frontier estimation.) It is unlikely that this pattern of inefficiency occurs, but it is also true that in our experience there is little gain from dropping the assumption of error independence across equations. For our sample of electric utilities, there are no large differences between Zellner-Aitken estimates and the estimates obtained by constraining error covariances to be zero; the extra information contained in the covariance between equations is small. In contrast are the changes that occur from imposing the cross-equation coefficient restrictions implied by Shepard's lemma: the addition of this information changes (for some coefficients) the magnitude and/or sign of the estimates. The assumption of independence between the cost and share equations is unrealistic, but it does allow the partial use in frontier estimation of the extra information contained in the cost shares.

Under this independence assumption the joint p.d.f. of the three disturbances is

$$f(\varepsilon_i, \varepsilon_{F,i}\varepsilon_{L,i}) = f(\varepsilon_i)f(\varepsilon_{F,i}\varepsilon_{L,i})$$

$$= f(\varepsilon_i)\left[\frac{|\Sigma|^{1/2}}{2\pi}\right]\exp\left(-\frac{1}{2}[\varepsilon_{Fi} \quad \varepsilon_{Li}]\,\Sigma^{-1}\begin{bmatrix}\varepsilon_{Fi}\\ \varepsilon_{Li}\end{bmatrix}\right) \tag{4-12}$$

where

$$\Sigma = \begin{bmatrix}\Phi_{FF} & \Phi_{FL}\\ \Phi_{FL} & \Phi_{LL}\end{bmatrix},$$

the variance matrix for the share disturbances, and $f(\varepsilon_i)$ is the appropriate p.d.f. for ε_i.

Because of the increased complexity of this model as regards estimation, we only present the likelihood function for the random variables $\ln(C_i/P_{K,i})$, $S_{F,i}$, and $S_{L,i}$ under the normal-truncated form of $f(\varepsilon_i)$ (hereafter denoted as SYS):

$$\text{SYS:}\quad \ln L\left(\ln\frac{C_i}{P_{K,i}}, S_{F,i}, S_{Li}\,|\,\underline{\beta}, \sigma^2, \lambda, \Phi_{FF}, \Phi_{LL}, \Phi_{FL}\right)$$

$$= -n\ln\sigma - \frac{\Sigma\varepsilon_i^2}{2\sigma^2} + \sum_1^n \ln\left[1 - F^*\left(1 - \frac{\varepsilon_i\lambda}{\sigma}\right)\right] - \frac{n\ln|\Sigma|}{2}$$

$$-\frac{1}{2}\sum_1^n [\varepsilon_{Fi} \quad \varepsilon_{Li}]\Sigma^{-1}\begin{bmatrix}\varepsilon_{Fi}\\ \varepsilon_{Li}\end{bmatrix} + \frac{n}{2}\ln\frac{2}{\pi} - n\ln 2\pi \tag{4-13}$$

Although this likelihood function was derived under the assumption of independence between cost and share equations disturbances, it is important to realize that adding the information present in the share equations does increase the knowledge of the parameters of the cost function; $\underline{\beta}$ is present in both the cost and share equations. This particular frontier specification does promise compensation for its complexity.

As is the case of the ALS single-equation models, the SYS likelihood function simplifies to a more familiar form if an inefficiency error does not exist. In this event $\lambda = 0$ and SYS becomes a constrained multinormal likelihood function, a Zellner-Aitken multi-equation model:

$$\text{Zellner-Aitken:} \quad \ln L\left(\ln\frac{C_i}{P_{K,i}}, S_{F,i}, S_{L,i} \mid \underline{\beta}, \sigma_v^2, \Phi_{FF}, \Phi_{LL}, \Phi_{FL}\right)$$

$$= \frac{-3n}{2}\ln 2\pi - n\ln\sigma_v - \frac{\sum_1^n \varepsilon_i^2}{2\sigma_v^2} - \frac{n\ln|\Sigma|}{2}$$

$$-\frac{1}{2}\sum_1^n [\varepsilon_{Fi} \quad \varepsilon_{Li}]\Sigma^{-1}\begin{bmatrix}\varepsilon_{Fi}\\ \varepsilon_{Li}\end{bmatrix} \qquad (4\text{–}14)$$

This model differs slightly from the typical Zellner-Aitken model in that the disturbances are restricted to exclude any covariance between the cost equation disturbances and the share equation disturbances.

4.3. Data and Estimation Procedures

Equation (4–1) describes the basic model to be estimated under the different log-likelihood formulations. The model is estimated using firm-level data consisting of 81 privately owned electric utilities. Firms included in the sample generated at least 75% of their output from fossil fuel plants, and operated with an average capacity utilization rate of at least 35%. That all the firms have similar characteristics is important, since the GAMMA version of the frontier is very sensitive to outliers due to the constraint that all the residuals be greater than zero. Due to the large number of parameters to be estimated, and the asymptotic justification for the assumed distribution of the estimates, we have pooled the annual firm data into three-year groups: 1964–1966, 1967–1969, 1970–1972, and 1973–1975. Thus, the sample size is 243 observations for each period.[3]

Equation (4–1) contains five variables: total costs, prices of fuel, labor, and capital, and output. Data for these variables are derived from various issues of the Federal Power Commission's (FPC) *Statistics of Privately Owned Electric Utilities in the United States* and the National Association of Regulated Utility Commissioners' (NARUC) *The Measurement of Electric Utility Efficiency*. Total costs are equal to the sum of expenditures for fuel and labor and imputed expenditures for capital services. Fuel expenditures and average fuel prices are obtained directly from the FPC and NARUC sources. Labor expenditures are held to be the annual sum of salaries, wages, pensions, and benefits. Average yearly wage rates are defined as total labor expenditure divided by the sum of the number of regular full-time employees plus one-half the number of part-time and temporary employees. Capital expenditures are calculated as the multiple of the deflated capital stock and the imputed capital service price. Output is measured as kilowatt hours of net generation. All prices and output are normalized by their sample period means. The definitions and derivations of these variables are described in fuller detail in Stevenson (1980b).

For each sample period we estimate frontier cost functions using maximum-likelihood techniques for the ALS-TN, ALS-EXP, GAMMA, and SYS versions. The parameter estimates from each of these versions is then compared respectively with OLS and iterative Zellner-Aitken estimates. The maximum likelihood estimates are computed with a program employing the iterative Davidon-Fletcher-Powell algorithm. (See Fletcher and Powell, 1963). Since this procedure requires the derivatives of the function to be maximized, we present the derivatives of the different log-likelihood functions in the appendix.[4] From the program we also obtain asymptotic standard errors for each of the parameter estimates; the program computes the inverse of the Hessian of the log-likelihood function, where the Hessian is calculated from the analytical second derivatives, evaluated at the converged maximum. Asymptotically the Hessian is equivalent to the information matrix, thus yielding asymptotically justified standard errors. In the case of the GAMMA version, however, the true information matrix is employed in place of the inverted matrix of second derivatives. (This matrix is presented in the appendix; due to space considerations we do not present the second derivatives for the other models.)

4.4 Frontier Estimation Results

The maximum likelihood estimates of the parameters of the four likelihood functions, together with the OLS and the constrained Zellner-Aitken estimates, are summarized in Tables 4–1 through 4–12. A quick inspection

Table 4–1. Coefficient Estimates for Sample Period 1964–1966

	OLS	*ALS-TN*	*ALS-EXP*	*GAMMA*	*ZELLNER-AITKEN*	*SYS*
β_1	17.636	17.467	17.519	17.365	17.602	17.442
	(0.020)	(0.016)	(0.019)	(0.011)	(0.015)	(0.023)
β_2	0.660	0.620	0.578	0.609	0.373	0.373
	(0.058)	(0.054)	(0.050)	(0.039)	(0.004)	(0.004)
β_3	0.149	−0.475	−0.511	−0.554	0.082	0.081
	(0.373)	(0.287)	(0.295)	(0.252)	(0.014)	(0.013)
β_4	0.269	0.297	0.306	0.329	0.095	0.095
	(0.072)	(0.066)	(0.061)	(0.049)	(0.002)	(0.002)
β_5	−1.764	−1.329	−0.691	−1.509	0.075	0.078
	(0.808)	(0.789)	(0.702)	(0.544)	(0.011)	(0.012)
β_6	0.743	0.512	0.471	0.559	−0.006	−0.007
	(0.343)	(0.321)	(0.313)	(0.231)	(0.008)	(0.008)
β_7	0.934	0.927	0.920	0.922	0.955	0.944
	(0.016)	(0.011)	(0.011)	(0.011)	(0.016)	(0.015)
β_8	0.075	0.022	0.002	0.023	0.144	0.102
	(0.028)	(0.023)	(0.023)	(0.019)	(0.027)	(0.028)
β_9	0.050	−0.105	−0.114	−0.100	0.014	0.013
	(0.063)	(0.047)	(0.051)	(0.043)	(0.004)	(0.004)
β_{10}	0.086	0.249	0.195	0.217	−0.012	−0.012
	(0.096)	(0.085)	(0.079)	(0.065)	(0.002)	(0.002)

Asymptotic standard errors in parentheses.

of Tables 4–1 to 4–4 reveals a general consistency in the various models' estimates of the coefficients of the cost function. Single-equation frontier models, ALS-TN, ALS-EXP, and GAMMA, yield $\underline{\beta}$ estimates that are very similar to the nonfrontier $\underline{\beta}$ estimates; and multi-equation frontier estimates (SYS) appear to be nearly identical to nonfrontier Zellner-Aitken estimates. Far more striking than the differences between the frontier and nonfrontier models are the differences between the single-equation models and the system or multi-equation models. The primary parameter differences appear to occur in the direct price terms. Essentially what the tables suggest by inspection is that there are two basic classes of estimators—those that incorporate the additional information present in the share equations, and those that do not.

This appearance of a close similarity between the frontier and "average" estimated cost functions can be formally tested. The OLS model is a restricted version of either ALS model, a restriction corresponding to $\lambda = 0$

Table 4–2. Coefficient Estimates for Sample Period 1967–1969

	OLS	*ALS-TN*	*ALS-EXP*	*GAMMA*	*ZELLNER-AITKEN*	*SYS*
β_1	17.855	17.703	17.767	17.368	17.839	17.680
	(0.017)	(0.027)	(0.022)	(0.037)	(0.014)	(0.024)
β_2	0.631	0.628	0.594	0.629	0.394	0.396
	(0.055)	(0.054)	(0.053)	(0.049)	(0.004)	(0.004)
β_3	−0.090	−0.060	−0.294	−0.068	0.107	0.106
	(0.415)	(0.393)	(0.392)	(0.372)	(0.017)	(0.016)
β_4	0.353	0.336	0.339	0.338	0.091	0.091
	(0.069)	(0.066)	(0.065)	(0.061)	(0.002)	(0.002)
β_5	−0.539	−0.751	−0.648	−0.792	0.059	0.061
	(0.519)	(0.451)	(0.470)	(0.464)	(0.008)	(0.011)
β_6	0.727	0.355	0.529	0.264	−0.0002	−0.001
	(0.321)	(0.364)	(0.314)	(0.287)	(0.008)	(0.008)
β_7	0.916	0.914	0.910	0.913	0.955	0.940
	(0.016)	(0.014)	(0.014)	(0.014)	(0.016)	(0.015)
β_8	0.033	0.029	0.024	0.032	0.103	0.076
	(0.027)	(0.025)	(0.025)	(0.024)	(0.027)	(0.025)
β_9	0.057	0.040	0.021	0.017	0.017	0.018
	(0.072)	(0.069)	(0.071)	(0.064)	(0.005)	(0.004)
β_{10}	0.087	0.085	0.093	0.091	−0.011	−0.011
	(0.097)	(0.094)	(0.094)	(0.087)	(0.002)	(0.002)

Asymptotic standard errors in parentheses.

or $\alpha = \infty$. Therefore, we can test the hypothesis that the two ALS models are equivalent to the least-squares model, and that SYS is equivalent to Zellner-Aitken. These tests of equivalence are conducted using the likelihood ratio statistics given in Table 4–13. By the likelihood ratio test we can reject the hypothesis of OLS equivalence at the 5% level for either ALS model for the periods prior to 1973. In the case of the SYS model, we can only reject Zellner-Aitken equivalence during the 1960s, at the 5% significance level. Thus, in spite of apparent coefficient similarities, there are statistically significant differences between frontier and nonfrontier estimates for most time periods.

Because the OLS model is not a true restriction on the GAMMA model, we do not formally test the hypothesis that both models are equivalent for our sample of electric utilities. An informal measure of the similarity between this particular frontier specification and least squares is available, though. As Greene (1980) shows, a close approximation to the ratio of GAMMA

Table 4–3. Coefficient Estimates for Sample Period 1970–1972

	OLS	*ALS-TN*	*ALS-EXP*	*GAMMA*	*ZELLNER-AITKEN*	*SYS*
β_1	18.226	18.082	18.145	17.452	18.212	18.077
	(0.019)	(0.025)	(0.020)	(0.013)	(0.016)	(0.036)
β_2	0.513	0.548	0.587	0.547	0.461	0.461
	(0.041)	(0.041)	(0.042)	(0.039)	(0.004)	(0.004)
β_3	−0.031	−0.259	−0.467	−0.270	0.117	0.116
	(0.178)	(0.186)	(0.191)	(0.169)	(0.013)	(0.012)
β_4	0.472	0.431	0.384	0.484	0.084	0.084
	(0.067)	(0.067)	(0.065)	(0.063)	(0.002)	(0.002)
β_5	0.229	0.275	0.241	0.369	0.051	0.052
	(0.565)	(0.517)	(0.485)	(0.528)	(0.008)	(0.009)
β_6	0.151	0.160	0.174	0.150	−0.004	−0.004
	(0.222)	(0.214)	(0.209)	(0.208)	(0.006)	(0.006)
β_7	0.938	0.922	0.917	0.918	0.962	0.947
	(0.018)	(0.017)	(0.016)	(0.017)	(0.018)	(0.020)
β_8	0.072	0.033	0.0005	0.031	0.106	0.085
	(0.032)	(0.033)	(0.039)	(0.030)	(0.031)	(0.030)
β_9	−0.056	−0.026	−0.003	−0.016	0.016	0.016
	(0.055)	(0.056)	(0.057)	(0.052)	(0.005)	(0.005)
β_{10}	0.324	0.317	0.297	0.323	−0.12	−0.012
	(0.096)	(0.096)	(0.095)	(0.089)	(0.002)	(0.002)

Asymptotic standard errors in parentheses.

standard errors to least-squares errors for $\hat{\beta}$ for large n is $(\rho - 2)/\rho$. As $(\hat{\rho} - 2)/\hat{\rho}$ approaches 1, GAMMA loses all efficiency advantages over least squares, and it becomes more likely that there is only a small difference between the increasingly symmetric gamma distribution and the normal. Over the time spans considered in this study, the value of $(\hat{\rho} - 2)/\hat{\rho}$ moves successively close to 1, ranging from 0.44 in 1964–1966 to 0.97 in 1973–1975 (see Table 4–8). This evidence suggests that the GAMMA frontier specification, like the ALS-TN and the ALS-EXP models, becomes indistinguishable from the nonfrontier model in the later time periods.

As mentioned in the introduction, it is of interest to consider nonintercept coefficient differences when comparing alternative cost functions. That is, we wish to determine if observed statistically significant differences between frontier and nonfrontier β estimates are merely a result of neutral shifts in the frontier down from the "average" cost curve or if the nonintercept coefficients for the various frontier cost functions are statistically different

Table 4–4. Coefficient Estimates for Sample Period 1973–1975

	OLS	*ALS-TN*	*ALS-EXP*	*GAMMA*	*ZELLNER-AITKEN*	*SYS*
β_1	18.869	18.797	18.811	17.662	18.858	18.857
	(0.015)	(0.046)	(0.021)	(0.011)	(0.013)	(0.567)
β_2	0.636	0.637	0.639	0.639	0.587	0.587
	(0.022)	(0.022)	(0.022)	(0.022)	(0.005)	(0.005)
β_3	0.264	0.262	0.258	0.267	0.159	0.158
	(0.076)	(0.075)	(0.075)	(0.075)	(0.009)	(0.009)
β_4	0.423	0.425	0.419	0.441	0.063	0.063
	(0.048)	(0.047)	(0.047)	(0.047)	(0.002)	(0.002)
β_5	−0.044	−0.072	−0.109	−0.159	0.045	0.046
	(0.284)	(0.284)	(0.284)	(0.282)	(0.006)	(0.006)
β_6	−0.232	−0.300	−0.226	−0.230	−0.026	−0.026
	(0.111)	(0.110)	(0.110)	(0.110)	(0.003)	(0.003)
β_7	0.927	0.925	0.922	0.923	0.939	0.939
	(0.014)	(0.014)	(0.014)	(0.014)	(0.016)	(0.015)
β_8	0.034	0.031	0.025	0.028	0.057	0.057
	(0.022)	(0.022)	(0.022)	(0.022)	(0.025)	(0.025)
β_9	0.0004	0.0008	0.002	0.002	0.008	0.008
	(0.022)	(0.022)	(0.022)	(0.022)	(0.005)	(0.005)
β_{10}	0.203	0.201	0.194	0.195	−0.008	−0.008
	(0.061)	(0.062)	(0.063)	(0.060)	(0.002)	(0.002)

Asymptotic standard errors in parentheses.

Table 4–6. ALS-TN Estimates of σ^2 and λ

	σ^2	λ
1964–1966	0.070	5.691
	(0.008)	(1.630)
1967–1969	0.052	2.211
	(0.010)	(0.768)
1970–1972	0.056	1.839
	(0.009)	(0.459)
1973–1975	0.024	0.743
	(0.007)	(0.560)

Asymptotic standard errors in parentheses.

Table 4–7. ALS-EXP Estimates of α and σ_v^2

	α	σ_v^2
1964–1966	6.62	0.006
	(0.770)	(0.002)
1967–1969	9.979	0.014
	(1.907)	(0.003)
1970–1972	8.137	0.014
	(1.063)	(0.002)
1973–1975	16.224	0.015
	(4.783)	(0.002)

Asymptotic standard errors in parentheses.

from the OLS or Zellner-Aitken estimates. One expects all differences between estimated frontier and nonfrontier curves to be explained by neutral shifts; because the error terms on the cost function are assumed to be i.i.d., the estimated slope coefficients are consistent for any of the error specifications used. Therefore, the nonintercept $\underline{\beta}$ estimates for OLS, ALS-TN, ALS-EXP, and GAMMA should only differ insignificantly from one another, and there should be no statistical evidence of non-neutral shifts.

Table 4–14 shows the likelihood ratio test statistics for the test of the hypothesis that nonintercept frontier β_js equal nonfrontier estimates. Inspection of the table shows that only for the first period does the imposition of such a restriction of the frontier model significantly reduce the value of the log-likelihood function. The hypothesis that the frontier nonintercept β_js are different from the OLS estimates is rejected for all three of the later periods,

Table 4–8. GAMMA Estimates of ρ and γ

	ρ	γ
1964–1966	3.569	11.468
	(0.171)	(0.943)
1967–1969	10.806	20.082
	(0.777)	(1.773)
1970–1972	21.990	27.762
	(1.858)	(2.489)
1973–1975	76.300	63.021
	(1.421)	(3.767)

Asymptotic standard errors in parentheses.

Table 4–9. Zellner-Aitken Estimates of σ_v^2, ϕ_{FF}, ϕ_{LL}, and ϕ_{FL}

	σ_v^2	ϕ_{FF}	ϕ_{LL}	ϕ_{FL}
1964–1966	0.035	0.003	0.0008	−0.0006
1967–1969	0.033	0.004	0.0008	−0.0008
1970–1972	0.037	0.004	0.0007	−0.0009
1973–1975	0.027	0.005	0.0005	−0.0009

for all three frontier specifications, by a log-likelihood ratio test at the 5% significance level. Thus it is only for the earliest period that the ALS and GAMMA specifications produce frontier cost functions with "shapes," as a function of input prices and output, which differ significantly from the "average" OLS cost function. This statement also holds true when we test the hypothesis that the higher-order coefficients for the frontier functions equal the OLS estimates; again it is only in the earliest period that one can reject the hypothesis of frontier and "average" cost function equivalence. (ALS-EXP for 1970–1972 is an exception to this statement.) Table 4–15 shows the values of the likelihood ratio test statistics for the test of this restriction on the frontier model.

A by-product of the maximum likelihood estimation is support for the existence of error, and thus cost increases, due to inefficiency. The estimates for λ and α, see Tables 4–6, 4–7, and 4–10, are significantly different from zero for all time periods, except for the last sample period in the case of ALS-TN and SYS. The fact that λ is estimated to be in the range of 0.7 to 6.0, and α in the range of 6 to 16, lends support to the notion of an inefficiency component to observed cost. Support for the existence and decline in

Table 4–10. SYS Estimates of σ^2, λ, ϕ_{FF}, ϕ_{LL}, and ϕ_{FL}

	σ^2	λ	ϕ_{FF}	ϕ_{LL}	ϕ_{FL}
1964–1966	0.063	1.777	0.003	0.0008	−0.0005
	(0.010)	(0.422)	(0.0002)	(0.001)	(0.0001)
1967–1969	0.059	1.663	0.003	0.0007	−0.0006
	(0.010)	(0.393)	(0.0003)	(0.0007)	(0.0001)
1970–1972	0.056	1.097	0.004	0.0007	−0.0009
	(0.011)	(0.385)	(0.0003)	(0.0007)	(0.0001)
1973–1975	0.026	0.004	0.004	0.0005	−0.0009
	(0.002)	(4.39)	(0.0004)	(0.0005)	(0.0001)

Asymptotic standard errors in parentheses.

Table 4–11. Expected Value of the Inefficiency Disturbance

	ALS-TN	*ALS-EXP*	*GAMMA*	*SYS*
1964–1966	0.21	0.15	0.31	0.17
1967–1969	0.16	0.10	0.50	0.17
1970–1972	0.17	0.12	0.79	0.14
1973–1975	0.07	0.06	1.21	0.00

Table 4–12. Variance of the Random Component of Cost

	OLS	*ALS-TN*	*ALS-EXP*	*GAMMA*	*ZELLNER-AITKEN*	*SYS*
1964–1966	0.026	0.047	0.029	0.027	0.035	0.031
1967–1969	0.025	0.024	0.020	0.025	0.033	0.032
1970–1972	0.030	0.031	0.028	0.029	0.037	0.039
1973–1975	0.019	0.015	0.019	0.019	0.027	0.030

Table 4–13. Likelihood Ratio Test Statistic for Test of the Hypothesis That Inefficiency Error Does Not Exist

	ALS-TN	*ALS-EXP*	*SYS*
1964–1966	28.4*	31.4*	9.42*
1967–1969	6.0*	5.8*	8.74*
1970–1972	7.8*	16.2*	0.0
1973–1975	0.2	2.2	0.0

*Significant at the 5% level for a chi square with one degree of freedom.

Table 4–14. Likelihood Ratio Test Statistic for Test of the Hypothesis that All Frontier Nonintercept β_js Equal OLS or Zellner-Aitken Estimates

	ALS-TN	*ALS-EXP*	*GAMMA*	*SYS*
1964–1966	20.8*	23.8*	25.2*	2.4
1967–1969	2.8	3.4	5.2	1.4
1970–1972	3.0	9.6	4.2	0.0
1973–1975	0.0	0.4	4.8	0.0

*Significant at the 5% level for a chi square with nine degrees of freedom.

Table 4–15. Likelihood Ratio Test Statistic for Test of the Hypothesis That All Higher Order β_js Equal OLS or Zellner-Aitken Estimates

	ALS-TN	*ALS-EXP*	*GAMMA*	*SYS*
1964–1966	13.6*	17.6*	15.4*	0.2
1967–1969	0.2	0.4	0.4	0.1
1970–1972	2.4	7.8*	2.6	0.0
1973–1975	0.0	0.4	0.0	0.0

*Significant at the 5% level for a chi square with three degrees of freedom.

measured inefficiency comes also from the GAMMA estimates of ρ (see Table 4–8). Over the entire period ρ rises quite dramatically, suggesting that while the cost function disturbance was originally very asymmetric, by the end of the period its distribution is very symmetric. The potential existence of inefficiency is brought out more fully in Table 4–11, where the expected value of the inefficiency disturbance is shown. Save for SYS in the last period, ALS-TN, ALS-EXP, GAMMA, and SYS all show nonzero expected inefficiency errors. This error appears to be declining over time for all error specifications.

The final question to be addressed is whether the estimated frontier functions show significant economic differences from the "average" OLS estimated functions. As mentioned previously, if the frontier estimation method yields minimum cost curves economically similar to OLS, the substantive value of frontier estimation in assessing the cost function is doubtful. In this situation the gain from using a frontier specification is low as compared to the computational difficulties of the approach. This problem is magnified when we consider the fact that maximum likelihood frontier estimation is valid only if the true distribution of the error term is reasonably approximated by the assumed distribution, e.g., ALS-TN or GAMMA. By using a number of alternative specifications we hope to have approximated the true distribution with at least one of the forms, and thus lessen the likelihood of this problem's occurrence. However, our choice of alternative forms does not exhaust the range of possible distributions.

Because the cost functions are multiparametered, direct comparisons of the economic content of the cost curves are difficult. If all measured differences were accounted for by estimated intercept differences alone, one could simply compare frontier intercepts to nonfrontier intercepts. However, the point estimates of the slope coefficients will vary from model to model, even though they are statistically indistinguishable from one another. These differences should be accounted for in any economic measure since the true values of slope coefficients are unknown; therefore, to compare the functions we need a single-valued measure that expresses the k-dimensional parameter differences between the functions. As one such measure, we propose the average frontier cost relative to the OLS or Zellner-Aitken estimated cost, as defined over a range of input prices and output levels. The ratio of estimated frontier costs relative to nonfrontier estimated costs for a given P_F/P_K, P_L/P_K and Q is

$$\begin{aligned}\hat{C}_F/\hat{C}_{OLS} &= \exp[\underline{X}'(\hat{\underline{\beta}}_{\text{Front.}} - \hat{\underline{\beta}}_{OLS})] \\ &= \exp[\underline{X}'\Delta\hat{\underline{\beta}}\,] \\ &= e^{\Delta\hat{\beta}_1} \cdot [P_F/P_K] \exp(\Delta\hat{\beta}_2 + \Delta\hat{\beta}_3/2 \ln P_F/P_K + \Delta\hat{\beta}_6 \ln P_L/P_K + \Delta\hat{\beta}_9 \ln Q) \\ &\quad \cdot [P_L/P_K] \exp(\Delta\hat{\beta}_4 + \Delta\hat{\beta}_5/2 \ln P_L/P_K + \Delta\hat{\beta}_{10} \ln Q) \\ &\quad \cdot [Q] \exp(\Delta\hat{\beta}_7 + \Delta\hat{\beta}_8/2 \ln Q)\end{aligned}$$

where $\underline{X}$ is the data vector for the independent variables and $\underline{\beta}$ is the parameter vector.

The average relative frontier cost (ARFC) equals

$$\text{ARFC} = \frac{\displaystyle\int_{P_{F1}}^{P_{F2}} \int_{P_{L1}}^{P_{L2}} \int_{Q_1}^{Q_2} \hat{C}_F/\hat{C}_{\text{OLS}}\, dQ\, dP_L\, dP_F}{(P_{F2} - P_{F1})(P_{L2} - P_{L1})(Q_2 - Q_1)}$$

$$= e^{\Delta\hat{\beta}_1} \cdot \frac{\displaystyle\int_{P_{F1}}^{P_{F2}} \int_{P_{L1}}^{P_{L2}} \int_{Q_1}^{Q_2} \exp[\underline{X}'_* \Delta\underline{\beta}^*] dQ\, dP_L\, dP_F}{(P_{F2} - P_{F1})(P_{L2} - P_{L1})(Q_2 - Q_1)}$$

$$= \text{ARFC}_1 \cdot \text{ARFC}_2$$

where $\Delta\underline{\beta}^*$ excludes $\Delta\beta_1$, and $\underline{X}'_*$ excludes the intercept.[5]

ARFC measures the average ratio of frontier to nonfrontier cost, and has two components. The first component, ARFC_1, is an intercept scaling factor representing estimated intercept differences between the frontier and "average" cost curves. ARFC_1 thus measures the degree of any neutral downward shift in the frontier. The second component, ARFC_2, represents that portion of relative cost that is a function of input prices and output. ARFC_2 measures average relative cost reductions due to non-neutral shifts in the frontier. Any nonneutral cost reductions should be minor due to the consistency of the nonintercept OLS β estimates. Differences in the estimates are not necessarily statistical artifacts since the frontier estimates are presumably tighter estimates.

Values of ARFC, together with ARFC_1 and ARFC_2, are shown for the four frontier specifications in Table 4–16. The values are calculated for two different ranges of input prices and output. The first range is defined over the sample minimum and maximum observations on P_F/P_K, P_L/P_K, and Q. The second range is defined over the sample mean of the three variables plus or minus one sample standard deviation. (This second range is a subinterval of the first.) For the first range, the frontier on average is 15% to 30% less than the "average" curve for the period 1964–1966. Such a reduction suggests great differences between frontier and "average" performance. Excluding

Table 4–16. Average Relative Frontier Cost (ARFC) and its Components, Intercept (ARFC_1) and Nonintercept (ARFC_2) Costs

	Range					
	Minimum–Maximum			*Mean + 1 STd. Dev.*		
	ARFC	*$ARFC_1$*	*$ARFC_2$*	*ARFC*	*$ARFC_1$*	*$ARFC_2$*
1964–1966						
ALS-TN	0.774	0.844	0.917	0.829	0.844	0.959
ALS-EXP	0.805	0.890	0.905	0.872	0.890	0.958
GAMMA	0.690	0.763	0.904	0.748	0.763	0.958
SYS	0.874	0.852	0.964	0.844	0.852	0.990
1967–1969						
ALS-TN	0.827	0.859	0.963	0.844	0.859	0.983
ALS-EXP	0.870	0.916	0.949	0.898	0.916	0.980
GAMMA	0.589	0.615	0.958	0.605	0.615	0.983
SYS	0.869	0.853	0.977	0.869	0.085	0.996
1970–1972						
ALS-TN	0.814	0.866	0.940	0.851	0.866	0.983
ALS-EXP	0.820	0.922	0.889	0.896	0.922	0.972
GAMMA	0.435	0.461	0.943	0.454	0.461	0.984
SYS	0.884	0.873	0.978	0.871	0.873	0.998
1973–1975						
ALS-TN	0.925	0.931	0.994	0.930	0.931	0.999
ALS-EXP	0.928	0.944	0.983	0.942	0.944	0.998
GAMMA	0.295	0.299	0.986	0.299	0.299	1.000
SYS	0.999	0.999	1.000	0.999	0.999	1.000

GAMMA estimates, as we move forward in time this reduction remains roughly constant until the last period, when ALS reductions drop to under 8%, and SYS reductions disappear. This result is consistent with our earlier evidence that substantial inefficiency error exists for all periods save the last. GAMMA ARFC falls continuously through time, eventually yielding an extremely high cost reduction estimate of 70% in the final period. This reduction is mainly of a neutral-shift character, however. $ARFC_2$, the non-neutral shift component of relative cost, increases over time for all frontier model specifications, including GAMMA. By 1973–1975 all non-neutral cost reductions have essentially disappeared.

Frontier cost reductions for the smaller second range are not as impressive as those estimated for the broader min-max range. For the earliest period, the nonneutral $ARFC_2$ cost reductions are only 4% as compared to 10% for the min-max range in the case of ALS-TN, ALS-EXP, and GAMMA. For SYS the smaller range only produces a non-neutral cost reduction of 1% in 1964–1966. In later periods the total non-neutral cost reduction essentially falls to zero for all models; while the total cost reduction is still sizable before 1973, this reduction is due solely to intercept differences. This sensitivity of the degree of non-neutral cost reduction to changes in the range of prices and

Table 4–17. Sample Mean Ratios of Estimated Frontier Cost to Estimated OLS or Zellner-Aitken Cost

A. Intercept Effect Suppressed

	ALS-TN	*ALS-EXP*	*GAMMA*	*SYS*
1964–1966	0.965	0.968	0.962	0.988
1967–1969	0.987	0.985	0.985	0.994
1970–1972	0.981	0.960	0.982	0.997
1973–1975	0.999	0.996	0.997	1.000

B. Intercept Effect Included

	ALS-TN	*ALS-EXP*	*GAMMA*	*SYS*
1964–1966	0.815	0.861	0.733	0.841
1967–1969	0.847	0.902	0.605	0.848
1970–1972	0.849	0.885	0.453	0.871
1973–1975	0.929	0.940	0.298	0.999

output suggests that the economic differences between frontier and "average" cost curves may not be great.

This suspicion is not decreased by an alternative method of comparing cost curve differences, the sample mean ratio of estimated frontier cost to estimated nonfrontier cost. This measure, unlike ARFC, is heavily influenced by the characteristics of our sample of electric utilities. Unlike ARFC, though, this measure does not have the problem of being greatly affected by nonlinear cost changes occurring at extreme values of relative prices and output. (As with any estimated model, confidence that the model adequately explains reality is greatest in the region around the sample means of the data set; this problem is exacerbated by the use of only a second-order translogarithmic functional form.) This measure shows evidence of a slight reduction in costs on the frontier that is not due to intercept changes. As shown in part A of Table 4–17, for ALS-TN, ALS-EXP, and GAMMA costs are reduced by 3–4% from the "average" performance in 1964–1966. For other years the reduction is smaller, and in the case of SYS there is only a negligible fall in costs for any period. Thus it appears to be the case that though there is evidence of sizable cost reductions in frontier performance relative to "average" performance, as expected these reductions are due only to intercept differences.

4.5. Conclusion

The purpose of this paper is to consider the effects of utilizing alternative frontier error distribution specifications on the shape and level of a reduced form cost function. Under the assumption that the residual of the cost-share equations (4–10) and (4–11) are multinormally distributed and are independent of ε_i, the residual of the cost function (4–1) the following conclusions are reached. The results indicate that for most periods the hypothesis of no inefficiency can be rejected. The effect of inefficiency on the cost curve appears to be, for most time periods, manifested in a downward neutral shift. The shape of the cost function does not appear to be significantly affected. Thus if one is interested only in determining the shape of the cost function, from which such information or scale elasticities can be derived, the use of frontier estimation procedures may well not yield sufficient benefits to equate with the difficulties involved. For other questions, such as the extent of inefficiency and the relative inefficiency of individual firms, the frontier approach may well be most appropriate.

Notes

1. However, normal random disturbances must be consistent with technical and allocative efficiency. Machine breakdowns due to poor maintenance are not compatible with the concept of a symmetric error disturbance.

2. This step assumes, of course, that the disturbances are i.i.d. As will be noted below, there is a possible problem with our sample on this score. This step also assumes that ε_i is independent of the explanatory variables. Because ε_i involves a disturbance due to inefficiency effects, this assumption could conceivably be violated, e.g., a utility pays unnecessarily high prices for its inputs into generation. For derivations see Weinstein (1964), and Meussen and van den Broeck (1977).

3. Since inefficiency errors might be correlated for a firm across time this procedure might cause problems since the ε_is might not be i.i.d. However, a correlation of about −0.1 of time with the residuals suggests that this potential problem is not likely to have any significant effect on our results.

4. Second derivatives, being long and tedious, are not presented in this paper. These equations are available on request, however.

5. In the case of the SYS frontier costs relative to nonfrontier costs, Zellner-Aitken estimates are used in place of OLS estimates.

References

Aigner, D. J.; T. Amemiya, and D. J. Poirier, 1976, "On The Estimation of Production Frontiers: Maximum Likelihood Estimation of the Parameters of a Continuous Density Function," *International Economic Review* 17, no. 2:377–396.

Aigner, D. J.; C.A.K. Lovell; and P. Schmidt, 1977, "Formulation and Estimation of Stochastic Frontier Function Models," *Journal of Econometrics* 6: 21–37

Averch, H., and L. L. Johnson, 1962, "Behavior of the Firm Under Regulatory Constraint," *American Economic Review* 52:1052–1069.

Christensen, L. R., and W. H. Greene, 1976, "Economies of Scale in U.S. Electrical Power Generation," *Journal of Political Economy* 84, no. 4 (pt 1):655–676.

Fletcher, R., and M. J. D. Powell, 1963, "A Rapidly Convergent Descent Method for Minimization," *Computer Journal* 6:163–168.

Federal Power Commission, 1964–1975, *Statistics of Privately Owned Electric Utilities in the United States.*

Greene, W. H., 1980, "Maximum Likelihood Estimation of Econometric Frontier Functions," *Journal of Econometrics* 13:27–56.

Leibenstein, H., 1966, "Allocative Efficiency vs. 'X-efficiency,' " *American Economic Review* 56:392–415

Meunsen, W., and J. van den Broeck, 1977, "Efficiency Estimation from Cobb-Douglas Production Functions with Composed Error," *International Economic Review* 18:463–476

National Association of Regulated Utility Commissioners, 1975, *The Measurements of Electric Utility Efficiency* (Washington, D.C.: NARUC).

Richmond, J. 1974, "Estimating the Efficiency of Production," *International Economic Review,* 15:pp. 515–521.

Schmidt, P., 1976, "On the Statistical Estimation of Parametric Frontier Production Functions," Review of Economics and Statistics 58:1976.

Schmidt, P., and C. A. K. Lovell, 1979, "Estimating Technical and Allocative Inefficiency Relative to Stochastic Production and Cost Frontiers," *Journal of Econometrics* 9:343–366.

Stevenson, R., 1980a, "Likelihood Functions for Generalized Stochastic Frontier Estimation," *Journal of Econometrics* 13:57–66.

Stevenson, R., 1980b, "Measuring Technological Bias," *American Economic Review*, 70:162–173.

Stevenson, R., 1982, "X-Inefficiency and Interfirm Rivalry: Evidence from the Electric Utility Industry," *Land Economics*, 58:52–66.

Stigler, G., 1976, "The Xistence of X-Inefficiency," *American Economic Review* 66:213–216.

Weinstein, M. A., 1964, "The Sum of Values From a Normal and Truncated Normal Distribution," *Technometrics* 6:104–105.

APPENDIX TO CHAPTER 4

ALS: $$\ln L = -n \ln \sigma - \frac{\sum_{1}^{n} \varepsilon_i^2}{2\sigma^2} + \sum_{1}^{n} \ln\left[1 - F^*\left(-\frac{\varepsilon_i \lambda}{\sigma}\right)\right]$$

$$\frac{\partial \ln L}{\partial \beta_j} = \sum_{1}^{n} \frac{\varepsilon_i x_{ij}}{\sigma^2} - \frac{\lambda}{\sigma} \sum_{1}^{n} \frac{f^*(-\varepsilon_i \lambda/\sigma) x_{ij}}{(1 - F^*(-\varepsilon_i \lambda/\sigma))}$$

$$\frac{\partial \ln L}{\partial \sigma^2} = \frac{-n}{2\sigma^2} + \frac{\sum \varepsilon_i^2}{2\sigma^4} - \frac{\lambda}{2\sigma^3} \sum_{1}^{n} \left[\frac{f^*(-\varepsilon_i \lambda/\sigma)\varepsilon_i}{1 - F^*(-\varepsilon_i \lambda/\sigma)}\right]$$

$$\frac{\partial \ln L}{\partial \lambda} = \frac{1}{\sigma} \sum_{1}^{n} \left[\frac{f^*(-\varepsilon_i \lambda/\sigma)\varepsilon_i}{1 - F^*(-\varepsilon_i \lambda/\sigma)}\right]$$

where f^*, F^* are the standard normal and the standard cumulative normal probability density functions, respectively.

$$\text{EXP: } \ln L = n \ln \alpha + \frac{n\,\sigma_v^2 \alpha^2}{2} - \alpha \sum_1^n \varepsilon_i + \sum_1^n \ln\left[1 - F^*\left(\alpha\sigma_v - \frac{\varepsilon_i}{\sigma_v}\right)\right]$$

$$\frac{\partial \ln L}{\partial \beta_j} = \alpha \sum_1^n X_{ij} - \frac{1}{\sigma_v} \sum_1^n \frac{f^*(\alpha\sigma_v - \varepsilon_i/\sigma_v)x_{ij}}{1 - F^*(\alpha\sigma_v - \varepsilon_i/\sigma_v)}$$

$$\frac{\partial \ln L}{\partial \sigma_v^2} = \frac{n\,\alpha^2}{2} - \sum_1^n \frac{f^*(\alpha\sigma_v - \varepsilon_i/\sigma_v)}{1 - F^*(\alpha\sigma_v - \varepsilon_i/\sigma_v)}\left[\frac{\alpha}{2\sigma_v} + \frac{\varepsilon_i}{2\sigma_v^3}\right]$$

$$\frac{\partial \ln L}{\partial \alpha} = \frac{n}{\alpha} + n\,\sigma_v^2\alpha - \sum_1^n \varepsilon_i - \sigma_v \sum_1^n \frac{f^*(\alpha\sigma_v - \varepsilon_i/\sigma_v)}{1 - F^*(\alpha\sigma_v - \varepsilon_i/\sigma_v)}$$

$$\text{GAMMA: } \ln L = n\rho \ln \lambda - n \ln \Gamma(\rho) + (\rho - 1)\sum_1^n (\ln \varepsilon_i) - \lambda \sum_1^n \varepsilon_i$$

$$\frac{\partial \ln L}{\partial \beta_j} = \lambda \sum_1^n X_{ij} - (\rho - 1)\sum_1^n \frac{X_{ij}}{\varepsilon_i}$$

$$\frac{\partial \ln L}{\partial \lambda} = \frac{n\rho}{\lambda} - \sum_1^n \varepsilon_i$$

$$\frac{\partial \ln L}{\partial \rho} = n \ln \lambda - \frac{n\Gamma'(\rho)}{\Gamma(\rho)} + \sum_1^n \ln \varepsilon_i$$

Information matrix:

$$-E[\ln L_{\lambda\lambda}] = n\,\rho/\lambda^2$$

$$-E[\ln L_{\lambda\rho}] = -n/\lambda$$

$$-E[\ln L_{\rho\rho}] = n[\Gamma(\rho)\Gamma''(\rho) - \Gamma'(\rho)^2/\Gamma^2(\rho)$$

$$-E[\ln L_{\beta j\lambda}] = -\sum_1^n x_{ij}$$

$$-E[\ln L_{\beta j \rho}] = \frac{\lambda}{\rho - 1} \sum_1^n X_{ij}$$

$$-E[\ln L_{\beta_j \beta_k}] = \frac{\lambda^2}{\rho - 2} \sum_1^n X_{ij} X_{ik}$$

$$\text{SYS:}\quad \ln L = -\frac{n}{2} \ln \sigma^2 - \sum_1^n \frac{\varepsilon_i^2}{2\sigma^2} + \sum_1^n \ln \left[1 - F^* \left(\frac{-\varepsilon_i \lambda}{\sigma} \right) \right]$$

$$\frac{-n \ln |\Sigma|}{2} - \frac{1}{2} \sum_1^n (\varepsilon_{Fi} \varepsilon_{Li}) \Sigma^{-1} \begin{pmatrix} \varepsilon_{Fi} \\ \varepsilon_{Li} \end{pmatrix}$$

where

$$\Sigma = \begin{bmatrix} \Phi_{FF} & \Phi_{FL} \\ \Phi_{FL} & \Phi_{LL} \end{bmatrix}$$

$$\varepsilon_i = \ln \frac{C_i}{P_{ki}} - \underline{X}_i \underline{\beta}_i$$

$$\varepsilon_{Fi} = S_{Fi} - \beta_2 - \beta_3 X_{2i} - \beta_6 X_{4i} - \beta_9 X_{7i}$$
$$\varepsilon_{Li} = S_{Li} - \beta_4 X_{1i} - \beta_5 X_{4i} - \beta_6 X_{2i} - \beta_{10} X_{7i}$$

$$X_{1i} = 1,\ X_{2i} = \ln \frac{P_{Fi}}{P_{ki}},\ X_{3i} = \frac{X_{2i}^2}{2},\ X_{4i} = \ln \frac{P_{Li}}{P_{ki}},\ \text{etc.}$$

$\frac{\partial \ln L}{\partial \beta_j}$, $\frac{\partial \ln L}{\partial \sigma^2}$, and $\frac{\partial \ln L}{\partial \lambda}$ are the same as the ALS case, save for the following additional terms:

$$\frac{\partial \ln L}{\partial \beta_2} \rightarrow -\frac{1}{|\Sigma|} \sum_1^n [\Phi_{FL} \varepsilon_{Li} - \Phi_{LL} \varepsilon_{Fi}]$$

$$\frac{\partial \ln L}{\partial \beta_3} \rightarrow -\frac{1}{|\Sigma|} \sum_1^n [\Phi_{FL}\varepsilon_{Li} - \Phi_{LL}\varepsilon_{Fi}]X_{2i}$$

$$\frac{\partial \ln L}{\partial \beta_4} \rightarrow -\frac{1}{|\Sigma|} \sum_1^n [\Phi_{FL}\varepsilon_{Fi} - \Phi_{FF}\varepsilon_{Li}]$$

$$\frac{\partial \ln L}{\partial \beta_5} \rightarrow -\frac{1}{|\Sigma|} \sum_1^n [\Phi_{FL}\varepsilon_{Fi} - \Phi_{FF}\varepsilon_{Li}]X_{4i}$$

$$\frac{\partial \ln L}{\partial \beta_6} \rightarrow -\frac{1}{|\Sigma|} \sum_1^n [\Phi_{FL}(\varepsilon_{Li}X_{4i} + \varepsilon_{Fi}X_{2i} - \Phi_{FF}\varepsilon_{Li}\varepsilon_{Fi}]$$

$$\frac{\partial \ln L}{\partial \beta_9} \rightarrow -\frac{1}{|\Sigma|} \sum_1^n [\Phi_{FL}\varepsilon_{Li} - \Phi_{LL}\varepsilon_{Fi}]X_{7i}$$

$$\frac{\partial \ln L}{\partial \beta_{10}} \rightarrow -\frac{1}{|\Sigma|} \sum_1^n [\Phi_{FL}\varepsilon_{FL} - \Phi_{FF}\Phi_{Li}]X_{7i}$$

In addition there are:

$$\frac{\partial \ln L}{\partial \Phi_{FF}} = -\frac{n\Phi_{LL}}{2|\Sigma|} + \frac{\Phi_{LL}}{2|\Sigma|^2} \sum_1^n [\Phi_{LL}\varepsilon_{Fi}^2 + \Phi_{FF}\Phi_{LL}^2 - 2\Phi_{FL}\varepsilon_{Fi}\varepsilon_{Li}]$$

$$- \sum_1^n \frac{\varepsilon_{Li}^2}{2|\Sigma|}$$

$$\frac{\partial \ln L}{\partial \Phi_{LL}} = -\frac{n\Phi_{FF}}{2|\Sigma|} + \frac{\Phi_{FF}}{2|\Sigma|^2} \sum_1^n [\Phi_{LL}\varepsilon_{Fi}^2 + \Phi_{FF}\varepsilon_{Li}^2 - 2\Phi_{FL}\varepsilon_{Fi}\varepsilon_{Li}]$$

$$- \sum_1^n \frac{\varepsilon_{Fi}^2}{2|\Sigma|}$$

$$\frac{\partial \ln L}{\partial \Phi_{FL}} = \frac{n\Phi_{FL}}{|\Sigma|} - \frac{\Phi_{FL}}{|\Sigma|^2} \sum_1^n [\Phi_{LL}\varepsilon_{Fi}^2 + \Phi_{FF}\varepsilon_{Li}^2 - 2\Phi_{FL}\varepsilon_{Fi}\varepsilon_{Li}]$$

$$+ \frac{1}{|\Sigma|} \sum_1^n \varepsilon_{Li}\varepsilon_{Fi}$$

5 A FACTOR AUGMENTING APPROACH FOR STUDYING CAPITAL MEASUREMENT, OBSOLESCENCE, AND THE RECENT PRODUCTIVITY SLOWDOWN

T. Woodward

5.1. Introduction

One of the conclusions resulting from early research on economic growth was the existence of a large residual in explaining the sources of the growth of output. While it amounts to a tautology to say that all output must result from some source, it is also fairly obvious that many of these sources of growth may never be properly identified or measured; and the difficulty inherent in this identification process has made it tough going for those who have set out to reduce this "measure of our ignorance."

Typically these efforts have consisted of revising, adapting, and generating input measures. These new measures are then included in new growth accounting calculations to compute the effect that they have had on the residual. In many respects, this is a hit-or-miss approach. There is little guidance for fingering in advance the revisions that will significantly refine the *technical change* measure.

The author acknowledges helpful comments by J. R. Norsworthy, John Tatom, Robert J. Gordon, Martin Neil Baily and an anonymous referee. The views expressed here do not necessarily represent the views of U.S. General Accounting Office.

For this reason, David and van de Klundert (1965) suggested an alternative procedure by which the sources of productivity growth could be identified. They emphasized an examination of the nature of technical change itself with respect to the pattern of its factor augmenting biases. This would, they implied, point to the likely sources of growth and, therefore, better target the revisions. In their words,

> . . . would it not be preferable to begin by establishing the magnitude of these effects before attempting to identify them with specific secular developments? In other words, would it not be sensible to start by trying to identify *the form* which the growth of conventional input efficiency has taken and then proceed to tackle the intriguing, but quite distinct question of the sources of such growth?

More recently the study of productivity growth has taken a different twist. Instead of seeking the sources of growth, research has increasingly focused on the reasons why it has slowed down. Yet, in the investigation of the current productivity slowdown, David and van de Klundert's insight has been forgotten. This paper attempts to redress this neglect.

It demonstrates the usefulness of biased technical change measures in distinguishing among competing hypotheses of the slowdown. Estimates of nonconstant annual rates of nonuniform factor augmenting technical change for the private nonfarm U.S. economy, 1948–1978, and the U.S. manufacturing sector, 1958–1977, are presented. In this presentation, a slightly different method of deriving these estimates—combining the work of Sato (1970), Binswanger (1974), and May and Denny (1979)—is introduced. Finally, the May and Denny framework for estimating factor augmenting change in a translog model is adapted to the disequilibrium translog model of Mohr (1980).

5.2. Explanations of the Recent Slowdown

The recent slowdown in productivity growth is now well established. The precise timing and magnitude of the shift is still a matter of dispute, however. This is due to the cyclical nature of productivity, which makes it difficult to distinguish a genuine secular slowdown from distortions introduced by the business cycle.

Two methods exist to account for this cyclical pattern. First, the data themselves may be adjusted to form a series on productivity growth as it would exist at potential output. This approach has been favored by, among others, Denison (1979). However, it can generate different results from different definitions of potential output. As an alternative, one can measure average rates of change in productivity between comparable stages of the business cycle. This latter procedure has been used by Clark (1978), Norsworthy and Harper (1979, 1981), and Norsworthy, Harper, and Kunze (1979). While it suffers from its own drawbacks, the peak-to-peak approach does not suffer as much from the ambiguities inherent in selecting a measure of potential output.

Using the peak-to-peak measures, the slowdown is evident in the period after 1965. For the nonfarm private economy, labor productivity, measured in terms of hours paid, grew at a rate of 2.68% from 1948 to 1965 but fell to 1.96% during the period 1965 to 1973. From 1973 to 1978 the rise was only 0.88%.[1] For the more economically meaningful total factor productivity measure, the growth rate depends on the capital measure used. Numbers prepared by Norsworthy and Harper indicate a drop from the 1948–1965 average of 1.94% to 1.06% % for the 1965–1973 period. During 1973–1978 it fell to 0.66%.

The performance of total factor productivity makes clear that the labor productivity slowdown is not due entirely to lagging capital formation. Indeed, from 1965 to 1973 the capital labor ratio grew faster than during 1948–1965 (Norsworthy and Harper, 1981). Depending on whose estimates are used, changes in the growth of the capital-labor ratio can account for only 17% to 26% of the slowdown in labor productivity in the nonfarm private sector from the 1955–1965 average to that of 1973–1978. Clearly, the recent slowing of productivity growth has come principally from sources other than reductions in the use of conventionally measured inputs.

A number of hypotheses have been advanced in efforts to explain the slowdown. Changes in the demographic composition of the labor force, increased expenditure on mandated pollution abatement equipment, increases in energy costs, and reductions in research and development relative to output are among the phenomena suggested to explain the slowdown.

Various methods of growth accounting have been used to test these hypotheses. New input series are constructed and old ones adjusted to incorporate the above phenomena. Typically the inputs are weighted by their share of final compensation to determine their role in growth. Computing the contribution of inputs both with and without the adjustments will yield the differential effect. One can then calculate the degree to which the slowdown in productivity growth is explained by the adjustment of inputs.

Results from this procedure have been generally uniform. The change in the age-sex composition of the labor force can explain 1% to 4% of the fall in labor productivity growth from its 1948–1965 average to that of 1973–1978; most of that effect occured during the 1965–1973 period. Adjusting the capital stock for pollution control can explain an additional 4% (Norsworthy, Harper, and Kunze, 1979; Denison, 1979; Kendrick, 1980). Including entry inputs in the total factor productivity measure indicates that only 4% of the slowdown in labor productivity growth from 1965–1973 to 1973–1978 can be accounted for by reduced growth in the use of energy inputs.[2] A more sophisticated analysis places the impact even lower (Perry, 1977). In spite the efforts of Kendrick and others, estimates of R and D inputs are not reliable enough to produce a credible estimate of their contribution to growth or the slowdown.

Where this share-weighting procedure can be characterized as a structural approach to identifying the causes of the slowdown, some researchers have opted for a reduced-form approach. This usually consists of regressing the rate of productivity growth against all of the sources of productivity. Dummy variables can be used to test the breakdown of the time series into periods of slower growth. Then new determinants can be included in the regression until the dummies become insignificant.

Siegel (1979) uses this technique. She concludes that 83% of the slowdown from the 1948–1965 average to that of 1965–1973 is explained by pollution control efforts. Moreover, 58% of the subsequent decline, 1965–1973 to 1973–1978, is due to the rise in energy prices. Rasche and Tatom (1981) employ a hybrid approach. In answering criticism of their earlier work (1977a, 1977b), they present evidence of the effect of energy prices based on the Perloff and Wachter (1979) data. Since the implied effect due to changes in the quantity of energy is small, they add a price of energy variable to the regression. The result is a combination of a structural model in the form of an explicit production function and a reduced-form model in the form of the ad hoc addition of a price variable. This yields a high estimate of the contribution of energy prices to the slowdown.

The rationale for this approach is clear. A change in energy use, for example, might involve only a very small proportion of inputs but nonetheless be associated with a large change in output growth due to its effects on other inputs. The advantage of the reduced-form approach is that the effects caused by a given factor are permitted to take on a significance beyond that dictated by its factor share, so that these secondary and indirect effects are included in the total estimate. The disadvantage, however, is that the result depends crucially on the specification of the model. All major contributors to productivity growth must be included in the regression. Otherwise the slowdown may be attributed to some cause merely because it behaved much the same way as the true culprit. This is a particularly serious shortcoming when one realizes that the whole problem to be solved stems form the lack of knowledge of what exactly determines economic growth.

There are several reasons why the full effects of pollution control and energy prices on productivity growth may exceed those calculated from the share-weighted procedure; these will be discussed below. However, given the two approaches, there is little to distinguish the more correct estimates. The two approaches do have one thing in common. They both take as their starting point the growth accounting approach that David and van de Klundert hoped to improve upon. Both of these methods first hypothesize the effect and then test for its magnitude. What is proposed here is that we first establish some idea of the magnitudes involved, narrowing down the possible sources of the decline in growth, then look through the explanations that fit the bill. In other words, instead of first providing some explanation for the slowdown and then checking to see if it eliminates the residual, it may be profitable to do it the other way around: examine the residual first to determine what types of explanations may account for it. The value of this approach can be well illustrated in the case of pollution control and energy prices.

5.3. The Trouble with Pollution and Energy

The difficulty in quantifying the effect of pollution control measures and higher energy on productivity growth is that their impact can go far beyond the decreased use of energy and the diversion of capital to pollution abatement equipment. The impact might also include a reduction in the effectiveness of other inputs. As an input, a pollution control device not only fails to increase measured output, but it may also reduce the amount that can be produced by a given quantity of capital input, just as emission control devices reduce the power and mileage that would otherwise be obtainable from an automobile engine. In many cases, preexisting capital equipment cannot be easily adapted to pollution control technology. It may be less costly to retire the capital early than to operate it within the law. Analogously, a reduction in the use of energy may also result in a reduction in the use of capital. When energy prices rise high enough, some energy intensive technologies may become economically unfeasible and the related capital equipment becomes obsolete earlier than one would expect from normal depreciation.

These changes in the input of capital will, of course, go unmeasured. Many utilization adjustments to capital stock data used in productivity studies are based on the business cycle. But reductions in the use of capital caused by pollution control and energy prices are independent of cyclical movements. Similarly, capital stock measures are based on depreciation schedules that quite naturally do not account for the effects of early obsolescence caused by mandated pollution controls or higher energy prices.

The lower estimates of the impact of pollution control and energy prices include only the direct, primary effects on productivity. The higher estimates, therefore, must assume something about the size of the secondary, indirect effects. Implicitly, these higher estimates assume not only that pollution control has directed capital resources from the production of measured output and that higher energy prices have reduced energy inputs, but that the effectiveness of measured capital has decreased as well. For the higher estimates (e.g., Siegel's) to be correct, it must be true that the effectiveness of capital has declined—presumably due to the fact that capital measures are overestimates of the true stock of capital, and that the utilization of capital is lower than indicated by conventional adjustment procedures.

Recent work by Rasche and Tatom (1981) and Bailey (1981) explicitly recognize this. In each case, it has been argued that, among other things, the sharp rise in energy prices resulted in the early obsolescence of some of the capital stock and that conventional replacement cost measures of depreciation failed to account for this. Bailey adjusts his capital series by a measure of q, on the assumption that financial markets are accounting for what the capital measures do not. Rasche and Tatom, as explained, opt for a version of the reduced-form accounting approach.

It is as an alternative approach that the David–van de Klundert insight becomes so useful. Biased technical change is a measure of the effectiveness of inputs. By estimating the variations in the rates of biased technical change for the various factor inputs one can find out if capital has, indeed, become less effective and if its behavior is consistent with the overestimation of capital input implicit in the higher estimates of the contribution of pollution control and energy prices to slower productivity growth.

5.4. The Relevance of Technical Change Measures

Technical change can be viewed as a change in the isoquant map of a production function. Neutrality refers to some aspect of that mapping that remains invariant with respect to the technological change (Sato, 1981). Thus, the change can be "neutral" in a variety of ways depending on its invariant properties. Hicks neutral, for example, where the capital-labor ratio under a given set of input prices remains unchanged as technological progress occurs, is but one kind of neutral change. For common types of change specifications, the shifts in the isoquant map are equivalent to a remarking of the axes. Hicks neutral change can be represented by changing the measures on both axes. Harrod and Solow neutral can be represented by remarking, respectively, the labor and capital axes alone. Remeasuring both axes by different scalars will produce the equivalent of what is called nonuniform factor augmenting technical change.

Thus, each of these forms of technical progress is equivalent to an increase in inputs. The only difference is that the quantity of the input does not rise, its effectiveness does. Hence, Solow-neutral and Harrod-neutral change are also known as capital and labor augmenting technical change since they add to the effectiveness of those respective inputs. They are also called biased technical change since the augmentation of capital is not the same as labor, as it is in the Hicks case where they are augmented at the same rate.

In most cases one is only concerned with the shift in the isoquant map. The equivalence to measurement changes on the axes is just a convenient expository-mathematical device for developing a model. Yet the equivalence also permits an examination of the measures themselves. If, for example, the measure we use for labor input were to change, it would appear that the effectiveness of labor has gone up or down depending on whether the new measure makes more man-hours look like less or vice versa. This would appear to be Harrod-neutral technical change.

The example is not farfetched. If one is only counting man-hours as the measure of labor input and the labor force becomes younger and less experienced, a decline in a real labor input occurs while the measured labor input goes unchanged. Labor effectiveness has decreased. A demographically adjusted labor input measure would avoid this problem. But one has a choice: it may be thought of as either a change in labor quality or labor input. The example makes this clear: if phenomena occur that make the measure of an input deviate from the actual input, it will appear as a change in effectiveness, some kind of input augmenting technical change.

A more relevant example is, of course, the case of pollution control and energy prices and their effect on measured capital input. If they have had a significant impact, it should have been through the reduction of actual capital input relative to measured capital. This would result in a decrease in the effectiveness of measured capital.

Thus, bounds can be put on the potential impact of these two phenomena. By tracking the rates of change of input effectiveness before and after 1965 (and 1973) we can look for evidence that the series on capital augmentation changed its pattern after one of these years. If the decline in productivity has resulted principally from a slowdown in the augmentation of labor effectiveness or fairly evenly from both capital and labor, the hypothesis that energy prices and pollution control contributed substantially to the slowdown will be rejected. If a large part of the slowdown resulted from the behavior of capital augmentation the hypothesis will be supported (though hardly proven). In any case, the measure can provide us with an idea of how much of the slowdown can be attributed to changes in the characteristics of various inputs.

5.5. Theory of Estimating Technical Change

Estimating technical change in a way that will generate these series presents some serious problems. The first difficulty lies in distinguishing the effects of technological progress from economies of scale. Shifts in the isoquants can result from either, making their simultaneous estimation impossible in many cases. Sato (1981,1982) has shown that this problem can be avoided by choosing a production function that is nonholothetic under the chosen type of technical change, that is, by making sure that the technical change specification used does not shift the isoquants the same way that scale economies will. Another approach is to use pooled cross-section and time series data. In the next chapter, Greene provides a good example of the use of "panel" data.

For this investigation, it may be possible to avoid the problem altogether. The goal here is not to measure the magnitude of the rates of technical change, but to look at their behavior relative to each other. The degree to which technical change effects and scale economies are mixed together will not alter these relative patterns.

For example, imagine that the effectiveness of labor inputs is growing at a 2% rate while the effectiveness of capital inputs is growing at a 0.5% rate. Assume economies of scale add an additional 1% to the growth of the economy. If scale economies are assumed to be constant for purposes of estimation, labor and capital effectiveness will both appear to grow at higher rates—3% and 1.5% respectively. The relative difference between the two is unchanged. Moreover, if capital effectiveness should decline relative to labor, it is still distinguishable from a decrease due to scale economies, which would reduce both series by the same rate. Hence, for the purpose at hand, the problem of distinguishing scale and progress effects can be avoided by careful examination of the resulting effective input series.

A second problem arises in deriving the augmentation series. Estimating constant rates of capital and labor augmenting change in the David–van de Klundert mode does not meet the requirements of the test proposed here. In order to make comparisons between the rate of capital augmentation after the slowdown and that which occurred before, the rates of technical change must be allowed to vary in the fashion of Solow (1957), Sato (1970), and Binswanger (1974).

However, it is impossible to estimate such biased technical change without a priori knowledge of the values of the elasticities of substitution. Moreover, if technical change is not Hicks neutral, estimating elasticities on the assumption of Hicks neutrality will bias the parameter estimates. Thus, one cannot use substitution elasticities generated from a Hicks-neutral framework to correctly calculate the series of biased technical change. One can estimate the elasticities if the rates of biased technical change are assumed to be constant or one can estimate the variable rates of technical change if the values of the elasticities are known, but one cannot estimate both simultaneously. This is the Diamond-McFadden impossibility theorem.

The procedure used here is a two-step process. First, the elasticities are obtained by estimating a cost function where the technical change proceeds at a constant rate. The rates of capital, labor, or other input augmenting technical change can take on whatever values the regressions generate. Thus, neither Hicks, Harrod, Solow, nor nonuniform factor augmenting change is assumed in advance, and any systematic bias that results from constraining the technological change to be one of them when, in reality, it is another, is avoided. The second step then uses these elasticities to generate series of technical change on a variable rate basis.

This, of course, does not avoid any biases that might result from technical change being something other than the specification described here. The possibility of that kind of bias is unavoidable. It is impossible to measure a shift in the isoquant map unless something remains invariant, and this invariance property must be assumed. The point of the two-stage approach is to make the estimation of factor augmenting technical change internally consistent. As long as factor augmenting change is to be estimated, it must be estimated from elasticities generated from a model that also assumes factor augmenting change of the same type.

This approach to the problem is virtually an inversion of the Sato (1970) procedure. Instead of using short-run variable estimates of biased technical change, as he did, to test the long-run reliability of production functions, here the parameter estimates from the long-run cost functions are used to generate the series of input augmentation with short-run variations. This inverted Sato method can be applied to a translog production technology by simply combining the earlier work of May and Denny (1979), and Binswanger (1974).

The cost function is estimated and all changes in output not attributed to changes of input are regarded as technical change. Taking information on the pattern of input price movements in conjunction with the estimated substitution properties of the cost function, the residual is allocated to each of the inputs. Each input share of the residual is the change in the input's effectiveness. If energy prices or pollution abatement regulations have rendered large parts of the capital stock obsolete, then the effectiveness of measured capital should decline more than the effectiveness of the other inputs.

5.6. The Cost Function

The transcendental logarithmic cost function is one of a family of second-order Taylor series approximations to an arbitrary cost function. It takes the form,

$$\ln C = \ln \alpha_0 + \sum_{i=1}^{n} \alpha_i \cdot \ln P_i + \tfrac{1}{2} \sum_{i=1}^{n} \beta_{ii} \cdot (\ln P_i)^2 + \tfrac{1}{2} \sum_{i=1}^{n} \sum_{j=1}^{n} \beta_j \cdot (\ln P_i \cdot \ln P_j) \qquad (5\text{-}1)$$

where i and j are inputs, P is the price of input, C is the cost of output, t is time, and the αs and βs are parameters determining characteristics related to factor shares and substitution elasticities.

If technical change occurs in an input augmenting way, the effective price of inputs will be diminished. If this diminution occurs at a constant rate, effective input prices can be expressed as

$$P_i^* = P_i \cdot e^{\lambda_i t}$$

where λ_i is the rate at which the input price P_i is diminished (this is a negative value), if technical progress occurs.

Substituting P^* for P and rearranging yields

$$\ln C = \ln \alpha_0 + \alpha_t \cdot t + \sum_{i=1}^{n} \alpha_i \cdot \ln P_i + \tfrac{1}{2} \sum_{i=1}^{n} \beta_{ii} \cdot (\ln P_i)^2 + \tfrac{1}{2} \sum_{i=1}^{n} \sum_{j=1}^{n} \beta_{ij} \cdot (\ln P_i \cdot \ln P_j) + \sum_{i=1}^{n} \beta_{it} \cdot \ln P_i \cdot t + \beta_{tt} \cdot t^2 \qquad (5\text{-}1\text{a})$$

where,

$$\alpha_t = \sum_{i=1}^{n} \alpha_i \cdot \lambda_i$$

$$\beta_{it} = \sum_{j=1}^{n} \beta_{ij} \cdot \lambda_j$$

$$\beta_{tt} = \sum_{i=1}^{n} \beta_{it} \cdot \lambda_i$$

If all λ_i are equal, then input prices are diminishing at the same rate; this is the familiar Hicks-neutral technical change specification. If all λ_i are zero except for labor, the specification is Harrod neutral, and so on.

Assuming symmetry among substitution parameters, i.e., $\beta_{ij} = \beta_{ji}$, and employing Shephard's lemma

$$\frac{\partial C}{\partial P_i} = Q_i$$

(where Q_i is input quantity), equation (5–1a) can be logarithmically differentiated to yield a set of factor share equations:

$$S_i = \alpha_i + \sum_{j=1}^{n} \beta_{ij} \cdot \ln P_j + \beta_{it} \cdot t \qquad (5\text{–}2)$$

where S_i is the income share going to factor i.

Differentiating (5–1a) with respect to time yields

$$\frac{\partial \ln C}{\partial t} = \alpha_t + \sum_{i=1}^{n} \beta_{it} \cdot \ln P_i + \beta_{tt} \cdot t \qquad (5\text{–}3)$$

This is the change in total cost due to technical progress. Constant returns to scale will imply

$$\sum_{i=1}^{n} \alpha_i = 1 \qquad \sum_{i=1}^{n} \beta_{ij} = 0 \qquad \sum_{i=1}^{n} \beta_{it} = 0$$

This, however, means that one factor share can be expressed as a linear combination of the others. Thus, one equation can be eliminated for the arbitrary factor g. This yields

$$S_i = \alpha_i + \sum_{j=1}^{n} \beta_{ij} \cdot (\ln P_j - \ln P_g) + \beta_{it} \cdot t \qquad (5\text{–}4)$$

$$\frac{\partial \ln C}{\partial t} = \alpha_t + \sum_{i=1}^{n} \beta_{it} \cdot (\ln P_i - \ln P_g) + \beta_{tt} \cdot t \qquad (5\text{–}5)$$

Observations of factor shares and input prices can be used to estimate the α and β parameters. Using the Solow (1957) definition of technical change, one can construct a series of the change in the price of output not explained by the change in input prices. This is expressed as

$$\frac{\partial \ln C}{\partial t} = \frac{\dot{A}}{A} = \frac{\dot{P}}{P} - \sum_{i=1}^{n} S_i \cdot \frac{\dot{P}_i}{P_i}$$

to provide the dependent variable in equation 5,

$$\frac{\dot{A}}{A} = \alpha_i + \sum_{i=1}^{n} \beta_{it} \cdot (\ln P_i \cdot \ln P_g) + \beta_{tt} \cdot t \qquad (5\text{–}5a)$$

The usual error terms can be appended to the equations to be estimated simultaneously for the calculation of substitution elasticities from the βs.

One problem with estimating the function in this form is that the conversion of the cost function to factor share equations rests on the assumption of immediate adjustment of factor inputs to changes in factor prices. Such a quick realization of equilibrium may be unlikely. Mohr (1980) has adapted the Nadiri-Rosen disequilibrium framework to the translog model. Factor quantities may respond only partially to price changes in this model.

Factor shares in this model are assumed to change in response to the difference between the shares as they existed in the previous period and the ideal shares that are consistent with the current input prices. The change in the share is some proportion of the difference and is a function of that difference for all input shares as given by

$$DS_i = \sum_{j=1}^{n} T_{ij} \cdot [S_j^* - S_j(-1)] \tag{5-6}$$

where T_{ij} is the adjustment coefficient for the change in share i dependent on the conditions relating to j. S_j^* is the ideal income share for j and $S_j(-1)$ is the previous period's share for j.

The ideal share S_j is given by the equilibrium translog share equations so that, with substitution of equation (5–2), the equation becomes

$$DS_i = \sum_{j=1}^{n} T_{ij} \cdot [\alpha_j + \sum_{h=1}^{n} \beta_{jh} \cdot \ln P_h - S_j(-1)] \tag{5-6a}$$

Since all shares sum to one, the changes in the shares will net out to zero. An arbitrary factor input g can be dropped, just as it was before. This yields

$$DS_i = \sum_{j=1}^{n} (T_{ij} - T_{ig}) \cdot [\alpha_j + \sum_{h=1}^{n} \beta_{jh} \cdot (\ln P_h - \ln P_g) - S_j(-1)] \tag{5-6b}$$

Mohr's specification was developed for a model with Hicks-neutral technical change. Respecifying it to include the possibilities of non-neutral change is relatively simple. For the share equations, the only change is the addition of a time term:

$$DS_i = \sum_{j=1}^{n} (T_{ij} - T_{ig}) \cdot [\alpha_j + \sum_{i=1}^{n} \beta_{jh} \cdot (\ln P_h - \ln P_g) + \beta_{jt} \cdot t - S_j(-1)] \tag{5-7}$$

The remaining technical change equation is somewhat more difficult to adapt. One will recall that $\partial \ln C / \partial t$ was approximated by the difference between the growth in the output price and the weighted growth rates of input prices. This calculation, however, depends on the equilibrium assumption. Thus $\dot{A}/A$ as defined by the earlier equation is not the real measure of technical change, which will now be noted as $(\dot{A}/A)^*$. Since $(\dot{A}/A)^*$ is not observable, it is necessary to rearrange and substitute expressions to obtain an estimable form of the technical change equation. Begin with,

$$\left(\frac{\dot{A}}{A}\right)^* = \alpha_t + \sum_{i=1}^{n} \beta_{it} \cdot \ln P_i + \beta_{tt} \cdot t \tag{5–8}$$

and

$$\frac{\dot{A}}{A} = \frac{\dot{P}}{P} - \sum_{i=1}^{n} S_i \cdot \frac{\dot{P}_i}{P_i} \tag{5.8a}$$

In addition, we know that

$$\left(\frac{\dot{A}}{A}\right)^* = \frac{\dot{P}}{P} - \sum_{i=1}^{n} S_i^* \cdot \frac{\dot{P}_i}{P_i} \tag{5–8b}$$

Thus,

$$\frac{\dot{A}}{A} - \left(\frac{\dot{A}}{A}\right)^* = -\sum_{i=1}^{n} (S_i - S_i^*) \cdot \frac{\dot{P}_i}{P_i} \tag{5–8c}$$

Then, with substitution:

$$\frac{\dot{A}}{A} = \alpha_t + \sum_{i=1}^{n} \beta_{it} \cdot \ln P_i + \beta_{tt} \cdot t - \sum_{i=1}^{n} (S_i - S_i^*) \cdot \frac{\dot{P}_i}{P_i} \tag{5–9}$$

For the ideal factor share, S_i^* one can substitute an equation drawn from applying Cramer's rule to equation (5–9) of the change in factor shares. For the simple two-factor case it would be

$$S_i^* = DS_i/(T_{ij} - T_{ii}) + S_j(-1) \tag{5–9a}$$

Solving for more than two variables will naturally complicate the system. Yet, it will add no more variables to the number existing already. Thus, no matter how many factor inputs are used, the technical change equation adds the necessary equation for simultaneous estimation. There are the same number of equations as in the instantaneous adjustment model with the addition of the independent variables, $S(-1)$, to provide estimates of adjustment parameters.

This procedure yields estimates of α and β for all inputs. If technical change is of the factor augmenting (or price diminishing) type, this will provide unbiased estimates of the elasticities of substitution. However, the input price diminution over time is expressed as a single constant rate—essentially an average. The variations around this long-term pattern provide the information desired.

5.7. Technical Change Series

Once one obtains reliable estimates of the βs, it is possible to move to the second step: estimating the rates of technical change. Following the work of Binswanger (1974), begin with the factor share equations of the translog cost function:

$$S_i = \alpha_i + \sum_{j=1}^{n} \beta_{ij} \ln \cdot \left(\frac{P_j}{A_j} \right) \tag{5–10}$$

In this equation technical change is no longer specified as occuring at a constant rate. At any given time, it changes at the same rate as the augmentation parameter, A_j. That is, A_j is the rate at which the effective price of input j is diminishing (or the rate at which the effectiveness of the input is rising). This may be rewritten as

$$S_i = \alpha_t + \sum_{j=1}^{n} \beta_{ij} \cdot (\ln P_j - \ln A_j) \tag{5–10a}$$

In difference form it is

$$dS_i = \sum_{j=1}^{n} \beta_{ij} \cdot (d \ln P_j - d \ln A_j) \tag{5–11}$$

Expressed in matrix form, this becomes

$$DS = B \cdot (DP - DA) \tag{5–11a}$$

where DS is the vector of changes in the factor shares, DP and DA are the vectors of logarithmic rates of change in input prices and augmentation (i.e., biased technical change) respectively, and B is the matrix of substitution parameters, β_{ij}.

However, since the changes in the factor shares sum to zero, the matrix is not of full rank. Again, an arbitrary factor input g is eliminated, yielding

$$DS_{(n-1)} = B_{(n-1)(n-1)} \cdot (DP' - DA') \tag{5–11b}$$

where DP' consists of the $d \ln P_j - d \ln P_g$ and DA' consists of the $d \ln A_j - d \ln A_g$.

The $d \ln A'$ are obtainable by solving

$$DA' = DP' \cdot B^{-1}_{(n-1)(n-1)} \cdot DS_{(n-1)} \tag{5–12}$$

This leaves all of the $d\ln A_j$ expressed relative to $d\ln A_g$. For the purpose of this study the $d\ln A_j$ are required by themselves. One more equation is necessary to solve for this. It can be adapted from the end product of Sato's equation (5–2) (Sato, 1970), reading in cost form as

$$\frac{\dot{P}}{P} = \sum_{j=1}^{n} S_j \cdot \left(\frac{\dot{P}_j}{P_j} + \frac{\dot{A}_j}{A_j} \right) \qquad (5\text{–}13)$$

and rearranged as

$$\frac{\dot{A}}{A} = \frac{\dot{P}}{P} - \sum_{j=1}^{n} S_j \cdot \left(\frac{\dot{P}_j}{P_j} \right) = \sum_{j=1}^{n} S_j \cdot \left(\frac{\dot{A}_j}{A_j} \right) \qquad (5\text{–}13a)$$

This provides all that is needed to solve for all of the $d\ln A_j$. An A_j series can be constructed by setting the index to one in the first year and cummulating the changes by

$$A_j^t = A_j^{t-1} \cdot (1 + d\ln A_j^t) \qquad (5\text{–}14)$$

5.8. Data and Estimation

Two data sets are employed. The first is for value added in the U.S. nonfarm private sector, 1948–1978. The second is for gross output in the manufacturing sector, 1958–1977. Both of the series were prepared by J. R. Norsworthy and Michael Harper of the Bureau of Labor Statistics (1979,1981). Details of the derivation of these data are contained in their original papers.

The value-added series has the disadvantage that the direct effect of energy prices on output is not provided by the data. Capital and labor are the only inputs used in an analysis of net output. However, since the purpose of the estimation is to obtain a measure of the change in the effectiveness of capital, changes in the price of energy are not really needed. The gross output measure, on the other hand, allows for the estimation of the direct effects of energy prices. However, 60% of the inputs are in the form of materials. Since these materials embody much of the labor and capital employed in earlier stages of production, the full dimensions of the slowdown, and the contributions of energy prices to changes in capital effectiveness may not be picked up. However, manufacturing might be expected to react to the rise in energy prices (and to environmental controls) more than the private nonfarm economy as a whole.

The equation systems described in the previous section are estimated using the iterative Zellner Efficient method. This is a constrained joint generalized least-squares method. It amounts to estimating a "stacked" regression by minimizing the trace of the residual covariance matrix. The procedure is iterated to ensure that the results are not dependent on the choice of which share equation is suppressed. Kmenta and Gilbert (1968) have shown that the iterative Zellner Efficient Method is equivalent to the maximum likelihood estimator.

Certain properties of cost and production functions are expected a priori. The cost function should be monotonic; it should be convex; and substitution elasticities should be symmetric. Since the translog does not universally satisfy these properties, it is necessary to test the results to make sure that the data lie on the economically meaningful portion of the function. Monotonicity is verified if all estimated factor shares are positive. The function is convex if the Hessian matrix of Allen partial elasticities is negative semidefinite. Symmetry has been assumed for the estimation. Thus, to test for it, the system must be reestimated without the symmetry restriction. A likelihood ratio is constructed from the maximum likelihood of the two computations. The test statistic is

$$-2 \cdot \ln(L_{\max}(\Omega)/L_{\max}(\omega)$$

where Ω and ω represent the constrained and unconstrained problems respectively. The test statistic is distributed χ^2 with degrees of freedom set equal to the number of symmetry restrictions.

For sectors as large as manufacturing or the private nonfarm sector one would not generally expect prices to be exogenous except insofar as these sectors could act as price takers on a world market. However, an additional stage of least squares with instrumental variables is not employed. Most earlier studies (e.g., Berndt and Christensen, 1973) indicate that this makes little difference in the results. Thus, the possibility of simultaneous equation bias is recognized but nonetheless risked.

Table 5–1 shows the results of the estimation for the nonfarm private sector. These were estimated in the disequilibrium framework. Tests for monotonicity and convexity are passed. The Durbin-Watson statistics leave some question about autocorrelation. However, the null hypothesis of no autocorrelation cannot be rejected at the 5% level of significance. The β_{LK} estimate implies an elasticity of substitution of approximately 0.4, not inconsistent with the range of estimates existing in the literature.

Efforts to estimate the manufacturing sector in the disequilibrium model were frustrated by convexity problems. Equilibrium values were used for the technical change series. The equilibrium model parameters pass the con-

Table 5–1. Nonfarm Private Sector, 1948–1978

	Regression Results	
	Equation 1	*Equation 2*
Dependent variable	DSK	Å/A
R squared	0.7578	0.0387
Standard error of the regression	0.0046	0.0182
Durbin-Watson statistic	1.2210	2.1177
	Parameter Estimates	
A_k	0.339	(311.18)
A_l	0.661	(606.20)
B_{kk}	0.1485	(7.47)
B_{kl}	−0.1485	(−7.47)
B_{ll}	0.1485	(7.47)
$T_{ll}-T_{lk}$	0.8417	(8.60)
$T_{kk}-T_{kl}$	0.8486	(8.57)
B_{lt}	−0.0030	(−5.78)
B_{kt}	0.0030	(5.78)
B_{tt}	0.0004	(1.15)
A_t	−0.0158	(−4.54)

vexity requirements when consideration is given to the confidence interval around the point estimate of the own-price elasticity of energy. The test for monotonicity is also passed. In all equations the null hypothesis of no autocorrelation cannot be rejected. The results are shown in Table 5–2.

In both cases there were symmetry problems. While most of the symmetry tests were passed, the t substitution parameters systematically failed to conform to symmetry requirements in both data sets. Hence, a cost function was estimated without the technical change equation, ignoring the α_t and β_{tt} term and requiring no constraints on the ts. Parameter estimates are taken from both symmetry constrained and unconstrained calculations and biased technical change estimated from both, the results from the unconstrained estimates are compared with those of the contrained to check the robustness of the results. The comparison is given in the next section.

Table 5–2. U.S. Manufacturing Sector, 1958–1977

	Regression Results			
	Equation 1	*Equation 2*	*Equation 3*	*Equation 4*
Dependent variable	SE	SK	SL	$\mathring{A}/A$
R squared	0.9616	0.9630	0.8337	0.0477
Standard error of the regression	0.0006	0.0025	0.0047	0.0112
Durbin-Watson statistic	1.7164	1.4343	1.3400	1.5887

	Parameter Estimates	
A_m	0.595	(210.77)
A_l	0.279	(127.85)
A_k	0.110	(101.79)
A_e	0.016	(54.77)
B_{ll}	0.180	(10.61)
B_{mm}	0.217	(8.45)
B_{kk}	0.066	(16.04)
B_{ee}	0.015	(8.35)
B_{lm}	−0.162	(−8.43)
B_{lk}	−0.015	(−2.28)
B_{le}	−0.002	(−0.61)
B_{mk}	−0.047	(−5.79)
B_{me}	−0.007	(−1.47)
B_{ke}	−0.004	(−3.36)
B_{lt}	−0.004	(−11.09)
B_{mt}	0.004	(9.95)
B_{kt}	−0.0002	(−1.52)
B_{et}	0.0001	(0.97)
B_{tt}	0.0005	(0.98)
A_t	−0.0084	(−2.38)

5.9. Results

The constrained parameter estimates generated the augmentation series shown in Figures 5–1 and 5–2. Annual index numbers are given in tables 5–5 and 5–6 at the end of the paper. Peak-to-peak average rates of change are bracketed in the figures.

Casual inspection of the paths of capital and labor effectiveness in Figure 5–1 over the periods 1965–1978 and 1948–1965 reveals a couple of interesting characteristics. First there has been a clear slackening of growth of the effectiveness of both factors of production. Second, apart from the expected cyclical distortions, the effectiveness of capital has not declined.

To fully examine the effects of the changing rates of augmentation of effective capital and labor requires a more systematic review of the relative growth rates of the two series. One way is to compute how the technical change index for each input would have increased had it continued to grow at its 1948–1965 pace. The total actual change in the effectiveness of capital by

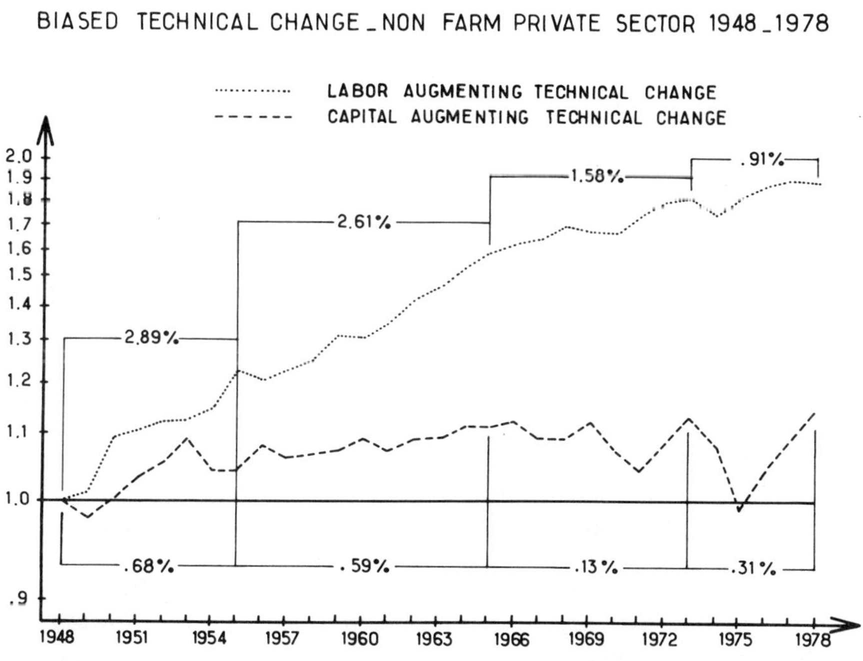

Figure 5–1. Biased Technical Change: Nonfarm Private Sector 1948–1978

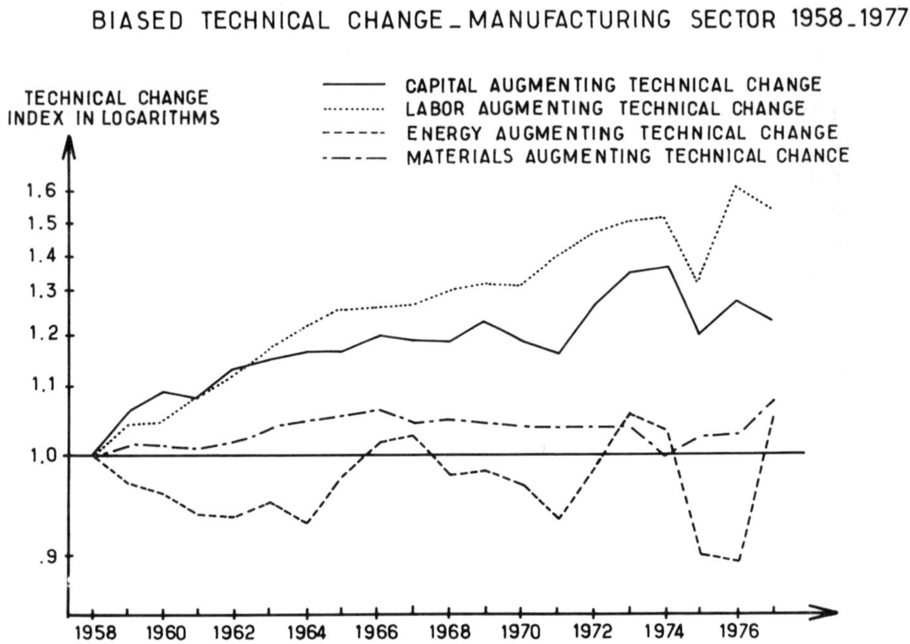

Figure 5–2. Biased Technical Change: Manufacturing Sector 1958–1977

1978 was 61% of what it would have been had the effectiveness of capital continued to be augmented at its preslowdown rate. The figure for labor, 73% was higher. The comparable figures for 1973 are more divergent. Capital achieved 64% of what it would have with no slowdown while the labor figure stood at 85%.

Again there is indication that the slowdown comforms to the Norsworthy-Harper decomposition into two stages. On average, for the entire slowdown, the slackening growth of the effectiveness of both capital and labor are not dramatically different. For the first stage, however, a slowdown in the growth of capital effectiveness contributed proportionately more to the reduced rate of growth of total factor productivity, while in the second stage labor played a greater role.

The extent to which these changes led to reductions in the rate of growth of total factor productivity can also be measured. Using equation (5–13) it is possible to calculate the percent of the slowdown due to the reduction in the rates of augmentation of the effectiveness of capital and labor. For the slowdown from the average rate of growth in the 1948–1965 period to that of

1973–1978, the slowing growth of capital effectiveness can explain about 9% of the slowdown in total factor productivity. Since the capital augmentation was contributing about 11% to the growth of total factor productivity during 1948–1965, this shows no disproportionate role in the slowdown for capital. For the first stage only, it accounts for about 20%. Labor is responsible for the rest.

The figures for manufacturing are less complete and, as a result, lend some ambiguity to the conclusions. 1977 is much further from the business cycle peak than is 1978. As a consequence, it is possible to only examine the slowdown in manufacturing through the first stage (to 1973); the figures for 1973–1977 are too susceptible to cyclical error to be accepted as reliable.

For the first stage of the slowdown, the growth of capital effectiveness was higher than in the 1959–1965 period. The cumulated change in capital effectiveness in 1973 was 111% of what it would have been if the 1959–1965 rate had continued. The cumulative increase in labor effectiveness was 80% of what it would have been if the previous rate had continued. Most of the drop was due to the slowdown in the effectiveness of materials.

The period from 1973 on might tell a different story if more data were available. Cumulative capital augmentation in 1977 stood at less than half of what it would have had the 1959–1965 rate continued. If this was not altered by events in the final two years of the business cycle it would indicate that the decline in capital effectiveness was crucial in causing the slowdown in total factor productivity in manufacturing during the second stage. But without another year of data it is impossible to judge.

As stated earlier, symmetry conditions for the β_t parameters were not met. Parameter estimates from both constrained and unconstrained versions of the model were used to calculate the augmentation series for comparison. Tables 5–3 and 5–4 compare the two sets of results. As one sees immediately, it makes very little difference in the results with the exception of the nonfarm private sector for 1965–1973. Capital augmentation is actually negative in that stage. This boosts the role of capital effectiveness to about 30% of the slowdown in total factor productivity for the first stage of the slowdown.

5.10. Conclusions

The pattern of growth of the effectiveness of capital and labor does not tend to support the hypothesis that either pollution abatement rules or the increased price of energy played a very large role in the slowdown of total factor productivity. Share-weighting the change in the growth of energy inputs also indicates only a small effect. According to some estimates, only

Table 5–3. The Effect of Symmetry Constraints on the Augmentation Series: Nonfarm Private Sector Augmentation Rates

	1948–1955	*1955–1965*	*1965–1973*	*1973–1978*
Labor				
Constrained	2.89%	2.61%	1.58%	0.91%
Unconstrained	2.86%	2.61%	1.72%	0.91%
Capital				
Constrained	0.68%	0.59%	0.13%	0.31%
Unconstrained	0.71%	0.60%	−0.22%	0.26%

2% to 4% of the slowdown in labor productivity can be explained by reductions in the quantity of energy employed in production.

The larger estimates of the contribution of these phenomena are generally derived from methods that do not depend on the share-weighting, or structural-form, approach. Siegel, who places the combined effects of mandated pollution abatement and higher energy prices at about 40% of the slowdown, uses the reduced-form estimation method. Rasche and Tatom, in their most recent work, use a hybrid method that explains virtually all of the slowdown in a single term appended to a conventional production function. In each, either implicitly or explicitly, it is assumed that transmission mechanism for these effects has been the rendering of capital obsolete earlier

Table 5–4. The Effect of Symmetry Constraints on the Augmentation Series: Manufacturing Sector Augmentation Rates

	1959–1965	*1965–1973*	*1973–1977*
Labor			
Constrained	3.16%	2.17%	.63%
Unconstrained	3.12%	2.25%	.55%
Capital			
Constrained	1.59%	1.92%	−2.55%
Unconstrained	1.67%	1.77%	−2.38%
Energy			
Constrained	.05%	.97%	.01%
Unconstrained	.28%	.60%	.06%
Materials			
Constrained	.63%	−.31%	1.13%
Unconstrained	.62%	−.31%	1.14%

than what would have been otherwise expected, making conventional capital stock measures overestimates of actual capital.

This overestimation of capital due to energy prices or pollution abatement standards should be reflected as a change in the pattern of capital augmenting technical change. However, the results generated by the estimation of biased technical change series do not come anywhere near these higher estimates. For the slowdown from the 1948–1965 average to that of 1973–1978 for the nonfarm sector, the growth of capital and labor effectiveness slowed about equally, indicating that capital did not contribute disproportionately to the decreased growth in the effectiveness of inputs. In the period prior to the slowdown, the augmentation of capital effectiveness contributed around 11% or 12% to the growth of total factor productivity; the remainder came from labor. From 1973 to 1978 capital contributed roughly the same or more to growth.

The only period in which the contribution of capital effectiveness to the slowdown is disproportionately large is from 1965–1973. In the first stage of the slowdown the slower growth of capital effectiveness was responsible for 18% to 30% of the slowdown in total factor productivity (the larger figure is drawn from the series based on the unconstrained estimates of the parameters). While this is 6 to 18 percentage points higher than the 1948–1965 norm it is still far short of the 83% contribution calculated by Siegel.

Results from the manufacturing sector also tend to confirm the conclusion that energy prices and pollution control had a small role in the slowdown. Declining effectiveness of capital played no role in the slowdown in productivity from 1959–1965 to 1965–1973. The important role of materials, which make up about 60% of the manufacturing inputs, also tends to support the notion that the causes of the slowdown were pervasive and widespread.

In many respects the use of this approach is seminal, and many improvements could be made in it. For one, more complete data series are already available. Extension of the series to the cyclical peak of 1979-IV is particularly important for producing more meaningful results. In addition, a more systematic method of comparing the relative contributions of capital and labor effectiveness would be extremely useful. The ability to find patterns in the relationship of capital and labor augmentation throughout the business cycle would make it possible to dispense with the peak-to-peak comparisons that constrain the region that can be examined. This would also make it worthwhile to use quarterly data with the attendant rise in the degrees of freedom.

A more sophisticated approach would employ a production function that is not holothetic under the chosen input augmenting technical change, enabling scale economies to be independently estimated. Alternative functional forms, such as CES, might be tested to see if a superior fit could be obtained. Alternatively, an even more general form of the cost function could be utilized.

It is worth pointing out that the technique employed here is different from that used by Jorgenson and Fraumeni (1981) for their extensive disaggregated analysis of technical change and relative prices in the U. S. They

Table 5-5. Biased Technical Change: Nonfarm Private Sector, 1948-1978

	Labor Augmenting Technical Change		*Capital Augmenting Technical Change*	
1948	1.0000		1.0000	
1949	1.0150		0.9867	
1950	1.0979	Average Change	1.0034	Average Change
1951	1.1093	1948–1955	1.0319	1948–1955
1952	1.1212	2.89%	1.0538	0.68%
1953	1.1264		1.0924	
1954	1.1482		1.0463	
1955	1.2238		1.0485	
1956	1.2018		1.0893	
1957	1.2295		1.0693	
1958	1.2506		1.0441	
1959	1.3105	Average Change	1.0703	Average Change
1960	1.3006	1955–1965	1.0984	1955–1965
1961	1.3441	2.61%	1.0787	0.59%
1962	1.4146		1.0959	
1963	1.4688		1.0998	
1964	1.5247		1.1117	
1965	1.5898		1.1125	
1966	1.6174		1.1201	
1967	1.6394	Average Change	1.0942	Average Change
1968	1.6963	1965–1973	1.0986	1965–1973
1969	1.6664	1.58%	1.1104	0.12%
1970	1.6626		1.0732	
1971	1.7344		1.0450	
1972	1.7966		1.0799	
1973	1.8047		1.1231	
1974	1.7330		1.0827	
1975	1.8139	Average Change	0.9987	Average Change
1976	1.8722	1973–1978	1.0494	1973–1978
1977	1.8943	0.91%	1.0929	0.31%
1978	1.8883		1.1405	

Table 5–6. Biased Technical Change U.S. Manufacturing Sector, 1958–1977

	Labor Augmenting Technical Change		*Materials Augmenting Technical Change*		*Capital Augmenting Technical Change*		*Energy Augmenting Technical Change*	
1958	1.0000		1.0000		1.0000		1.0000	
1959	1.0434		1.0147		1.0553		0.9771	
1960	1.0526		1.0112		1.0881		0.9764	Average Change
1961	1.0820	Average Change	1.0059	Average Change	1.0836	Average Change	0.9468	Average Cahnge
1962	1.1200	1959–1965:	1.0182	1959–1965:	1.1315	1959–1965:	0.9416	1959–1965:
1963	1.1769	3.16%	1.0343	0.63%	1.1473	1.59%	0.9578	0.05%
1964	1.2262		1.0460		1.1607		0.9389	
1965	1.2614		1.0537		1.1614		0.9800	
1966	1.2547		1.0621		1.1870		1.0163	
1967	1.2686		1.0451		1.1834		1.0296	
1968	1.3131	Average Change	1.0465	Average Change	1.1845	Average Change	0.9849	Average Change
1969	1.3181	1965–1973:	1.0433	1965–1973	1.2314	1965–1973:	0.9871	1965–1973
1970	1.3141	2.17%	1.0381	−0.31%	1.1844	1.92%	0.9727	0.97%
1971	1.4060		1.0298		1.1649		0.9413	
1972	1.4789		1.0300		1.2555		0.9893	
1973	1.5007		1.0278		1.3533		1.0593	
1974	1.5091		0.9985		1.3600		1.0367	
1975	1.3218	Average Change	1.0261	Average Change	1.2020	Average Change	0.9071	Average Change
1976	1.6048	1973–1977:	1.0299	1973–1977	1.2680	1973–1977:	0.8909	1973–1977
1977	1.5392	0.63%	1.0756	1.13%	1.2220	−2.55%	1.0587	0.01%

estimate a similar model of a transog cost function with biased technical change for each of 35 industrial sectors, but carry their work through the equivalent of the first stage of the estimation procedure used here. Since they hold the rates of input augmentation constant throughout, technical change varies year to year only in response to shifts in share weights. However technical change responds to variations in the rate of augmentation as well as changes in factor shares. Their conclusion that energy prices affected technical change is, in this sense constrained to factor share variations. As Table 5–2 demonstrates, 4.8 per cent of the variation in technical change can be explained by factor share movements if aggregate data are used.[3] Thus while they have demonstrated the direction of the effect of energy prices on technical change, the magnitude can be still quite small.

It is interesting to note that while the early-obsolescence hypothesis is rejected here, Baily, testing for it with his q approach, concludes the opposite. It may very well be that the only way to settle this question might be to use the Hulten-Wykoff method of measuring economic depreciation to determine if the age profiles of energy intensive equipment have reflected the energy price increase through faster depreciation and premature retirement.

Notes

1. While 1978 is not a business-cycle peak, 1979 is. Data were only available through 1978 for the nonfarm private sector and through 1977 for manufacturing. Since 1979 levels of economic activity hovered near 1978 levels, the 1978 figures can be taken to be sufficiently undistorted for use here.
2. Using the energy, capital, and labor series of Perloff and Wachter (1979).
3. This figure may be much larger if Jorgenson-Traumeni data are used. The disaggregated analysis might yield different results.

References

Abramovitz, M., 1956, "Resource and Output Trends in the United States Since 1870," National Bureau of Economic Research Occasional Paper 52, New York: NBER.

Abramovitz, M., 1962, "Economic Growth in the United States, a Review Article," *American Economic Review*, 52, no. 4: 762–782.

Allen, R. G. D., 1938, *Mathematical Analysis for Economists* New York: St. Martin's Press.

Arrow, K.; H. Chenery; B. Minhas; and R. Solow, 1961, "Capital-Labor Substitution and Economic Efficiency," *Review of Economics and Statistics* 43, no. 3: 225–250.

Baily, M. N., 1981, "Productivity and the Services of Capital and Labor," *Brookings Papers on Economic Activity*, 1981 (1), pp. 1–65.

Bechmann, M., and R. Sato, 1969, "Aggregate Production Functions and Types of Technical Progress: A Statistical Analysis," *American Economic Review* 59, no. 1: 88–101.

Berndt, E. R., and L. R. Christensen (1973), "The Internal Structure of Functional Relationships: Separability, Substitution and Aggregation," *Review of Economic Studies*, July, Vol. 40, pp. 403–410.

Binswanger, H. P., 1974, "The Measurement of Technical Change Biases with Many Factors of Production," *American Economic Review* 64, 6: 964–976.

Christensen, L., and D. W. Jorgenson, 1969, "The Measurement of U. S. Real Capital Input, 1929–1967," *Review of Income and Wealth*, Series 15, December, pp. 293–320.

Christensen, L., and D. W. Jorgenson, 1970, "U. S. Real Product and Real Factor Input, 1929–1967," *Review of Income and Wealth*, ser. 16, March, pp. 19–50.

Christensen, L.; D. W. Jorgenson; and L. Lau, 1973, "Transcendental Logarithmic Production Frontiers," *Review of Economics and Statistics* 55, no. 1: 28–45.

Clark, P. K., 1978, "Capital Formation and the Recent Productivity Slowdown," *Journal of Finance* 33, no. 3: 965–975.

David, P., and Th. van de Klundert, 1965, "Biased Efficiency Growth and Capital-Labor Substitution in the U. S., 1899–1960," *American Economic Review* 55, no. 3: 357–394.

Denison, E. F., 1979, *Accounting for Slower Economic; The United States in the 1970's* Washington, D. C.: Brookings Institute.

Greene, W. H., 1982, "Simultaneous Estimation of Factor Substitution, Economies of Scale, Productivity and Non-Neutral Technological Change," in A. Dogramaci, ed., *Developments in Econometric Analyses of Productive Efficiency* Boston: Kluwer–Nijhoff.

Hudson, E. A., and D. W. Jorgenson, 1978, "Energy Prices and the U. S. Economy 1972–1976," *Data Resources Review*, September 1978, pp. 1.24–1.37.

Jorgenson, D. W. and B. Fraumeni (1981), "Substitution and Technical Change in Production," *in Modelling and Measuring Natural Resource Substitution*, eds. E. R. Berndt and B. C. Field, MIT Press.

Ioannides, Y. M., and M. C. Caramanis, 1979, "Capital-Labor Substitution in a Developing Country: The Case of Greece," *European Economic Review* 12: 101–110.

Kalt, J., 1978, "Technological Change and Factor Substitution in the United States, 1929–1967," *International Economic Review* 19, no. 3: 761–775.

Kendrick, J. W., 1980, "Productivity Trends and the Recent Slowdown: Historical Perspective, Causal Factors, and Policy Options," in W. Fellner, ed., *Contemporary Economic Problems*, Washington, D. C.: American Enterprise Institute.

Kmenta, J., and R. F. Gilbert, 1968, "Small Sample Properties of Alternative Estimators of Seemingly Unrelated Regressions," *Journal of the American Statistical Association* 1180–1200.

May, J. D., and M. Denny, 1979, "Factor Augmenting Technical Progress in U. S. Manufacturing," *International Economic Review* 20, no. 3: 759–774.

Mohr, M., 1980, "The Long Term Structure of Production, Factor Demand, and

Productivity in U. S. Manufacturing Industries," in J. Kendrick and B. Vaccara, eds., *New Developments in Productivity Measurement and Analysis* Univ. of Chicago Press.

Nadiri, M. I., and S. Rosen, 1969, "Interrelated Factor Demand Functions," *American Economic Review* 59, no. 5: 457–471.

Norsworthy, J. R., and M. Harper, 1979, "Productivity Growth in Manufacturing in the 1980's: Labor, Capital, and Energy," Proceedings of the Business and Economic Section of the American Statistical Association, pages 17–26.

Norsworthy, J. R., and M. Harper, 1981, "The Role of Capital Formation in the Recent Productivity Slowdown," in A. Dogramaci and N. R. Adam, eds., *Aggregate and Industry Level Productivity Analysis* Boston: Martinus Nijhoff.

Norsworthy, J. R.; M. Harper; and K. Kunze, 1979, "The Slowdown in Productivity Growth: Analysis of Some Contributing Factors," *Brookings Papers on Economic Activity* 2: 387–421.

Perloff, J. M., and M. L. Wachter, 1979, "A Production Function-Nonaccelerating Inflation Approach to Potential Output: Is Measured Potential Output Too High?" *Journal of Monetary Economics*, supplement no. 10.

Perry, G. L., 1977, "Potential Output, Recent Issues and Present Trends," in Center for the Study of American Business, "U. S. Productive Capacity: Estimating the Utilization Gap," Working Paper 23, Brookings Reprint Series, no. 336, pp. 1–20.

Rasche, R. H., and J. A. Tatom, 1977a, "The Effects of New Energy Regime on Economic Capacity, Production, and Prices," *Federal Reserve Bank of St. Louis Review*, May 1977, pp. 2–12.

Rasche, R. H., and J. A. Tatom, 1977b, "Energy Resources and Potential GNP," *Federal Reserve Bank of St. Louis Review*, June 1977, pp. 10–24.

Rasche, R. H., and J. A. Tatom, 1981, "Energy Price Shocks, Aggregate Supply, and Monetary Policy; The Theory and the International Evidence," *Carnegie-Rochester Conference Series on Public Policy* 14: 9–94.

Sato, R., 1970, "The Estimation of Biased Technical Progress and the Production Function," *International Economic Review* 11: no. 2: 179–208.

Sato, R., 1981, *Theory of Technical Change and Economic Invariance; An Application of Lie Groups* New York: Academic Press.

Sato, R., and P. S. Calem, 1982, "Lie Group Methods and the Theory of Estimating Total Factor Productivity," in A. Dogramaci, ed., *Developments in Econometric Analyses of Productive Efficiency* Boston: Kluwer–Nijhoff.

Siegel, R., 1979, "Why Has Productivity Slowed Down?" *Data Resources Review*, March 1979, pp. 1.59–1.65.

Solow, R. M., 1957, "Technical Change and the Aggregate Production Function," *Review of Economics and Statistics* 39, no. 3: 312–320.

Tatom, J. A., 1979, "Energy Prices and Capital Formation," *Federal Reserve Bank of St. Louis Review*, May 1979, pp. 2–9.

6 SIMULTANEOUS ESTIMATION OF FACTOR SUBSTITUTION, ECONOMIES OF SCALE, PRODUCTIVITY, AND NON-NEUTRAL TECHNICAL CHANGE

W. H. Greene

6.1. Introduction

Several authors have studied the problem of simultaneous statistical estimation of scale economies, factor substitution, and technological change. Some very crude results appear in Christensen and Greene (1976). A framework for analysis is described in Christensen (1977) who extends the translog function to a time series setting. The most detailed aggregated study of which we are aware is that of Berndt and Khaled (1979) who propose a very general functional form for estimation, which subsumes numerous flexible functional forms as special cases, and show how various measures of technological change may be computed. Førsund and Hjalmarsson (1979) have studied scale and technological change effects in Swedish dairy production using a methodology very similar to ours. Their's differs from our's in that they use the notion of a frontier production function, and employ a nonstatistical estimation technique. (See their study, p. 885). Førsund and Hjalmarsson approach the analysis from the production side, rather than the cost side as we do; but their means of parameterizing technical change is basically the same as ours. In the previous chapter, Woodward used a slightly more limited approach. He assumed constant returns to scale, and studied scale and substitution effects using a method closely related to the one we discuss in section 6.3. Finally, we can cite Stevenson (1980) who extended the translog cost function methodology of Christensen and Greene (1976) in a way that greatly facilitates estimation of the various elasticities.

The literature contains several interesting papers—for example, Diamond, McFadden, and Rodriguez (1978); Sato (1970); and Sato and Calem (1981)—on the question of whether the simultaneous effects of economies of scale and non-neutral technological change can be disentangled empirically. In the next chapter, Sato and Calem show that in the setting of holothetic technology (see Chapter 7) the answer is no. Moreover, when using a "panel" data set as we do, one can, in principle, hold the technology (as far as time progression is concerned) fixed and examine scale and substitution effects even assuming the technology is homothetic. In sum, the Diamond-McFadden impossibility results apply only to time series analyses of rather restricted technologies. We note, finally, the intriguing means by which Woodward (in chapter 5) deals with the same problem. At the end of section 5.5 he notes, "if technical change is not Hicks neutral, estimating elasticities on the assumption of Hicks neutrality will bias the parameter estimates. Thus, one cannot use substitution elasticities generated from a Hicks-neutral framework to correctly calculate the series of biased technical change. One can estimate the elasticities if the rates of biased technical change are assumed to be constant or one can estimate the variable rates of technical change if the values of the elasticities are known, but one cannot estimate both simultaneously." He takes a two-step approach, first estimating a cost function to produce elasticity estimates assuming a constant rate of technical change but variable rates of input augmentation, then, second, using the elasticities "to generate series of technical change on a variable rate basis."

This paper presents two sets of results. First, we obtain some general results on decomposing changes in costs and factor demands over time into scale, substitution, and technological change effects. The sources of change in cost are described in Christensen (1977). Stevenson (1980) gives some discussion of the second; we have extended his analysis in a couple of directions and derived easily interpreted (and quantified) measures of the effects on factor demands of factor biased technological change.

The second result in the paper concerns estimation methodology. The Berndt and Khaled (1979) study presents an extremely flexible model and a method for estimating many interesting elasticities. However, the computational burden of estimation in their model is substantial to say the least, and as amply shown by Stevenson, one can achieve almost the same end at a fraction of the cost. Stevenson proposes a much simpler framework for analysis, but stops short of Berndt and Khaled in the interpretation of the results. This paper falls somewhat between these two studies.

Our estimation technique is, after some rearrangement, substantially similar to Stevensons. We find this to be a very convenient means of analyzing rates of change of cost and factor demands. We have extended the methodology to the decomposition of rates of change in the factor demands. Finally, we are able to estimate differential technological effects over several different periods.

The methodology is applied to a 20-year (5-year intervals) panel data set from the electric power industry. Our findings differ sharply from Stevenson's in some respects, but are largely the same in others. The primary difference lies in our considerably higher estimates of the pace of technological change in the industry.

6.2. Specification

The characteristics of technology that we wish to analyze are economies of scale, factor substitution, and technological change. Direct estimation of the production function is a logical way to proceed; however, the results of a number of studies (e.g., Berndt and Khaled, 1979, and Christensen and Greene, 1976) have shown that the neoclassical cost function approach is much more convenient.

We assume, then, that production is characterized by a production function satisfying the usual regularity conditions,

$$y = f(x, t)$$

The arguments of the function are a vector of M inputs, x, and time, t, which indicates the effect of technological change. Output is denoted by y. Assuming that input prices, p, are determined exogenously, the dual cost function may be written

$$c = c(y, p, t)$$

The use of the cost function to analyze economies of scale is discussed in Hanoch (1975) and Christensen and Greene (1976). The ratio of marginal cost to average cost at any point on the cost function,

$$\varepsilon = \frac{\partial c/\partial y}{c/y} = \frac{\partial \log c}{\partial \log y}$$

gives a measure of the economies of scale available at output y. Values of ε less than one imply scale economies and values greater than one imply diseconomies. Various authors have employed modifications of this measure; for example, Ohta (1974) and Berndt and Khaled (1979) define the dual rate of returns to scale as $1/\varepsilon$, while Christensen and Greene (1976) define scale economies, SCE, as $1 - \varepsilon$. The production function is homothetic if and only if ε is independent of p, homogeneous if and only if ε is independent of both $\bar{p}$ and y, and linearly homogeneous if and only if $\varepsilon = 1$.

Allen elasticities of substitution may be computed easily from the cost function using

$$\sigma_{ij} = \frac{[\partial^2 c/(\partial p_i \, \partial p_j)]c}{(\partial c/\partial p_i)\,(\partial c/\partial p_j)}$$

There are numerous ways in which technical change may be specified. Christensen (1977) analyzes several possibilities, the simplest being Hicks neutral. Other specifications involve the modelling of constant rates of factor augmentation or factor price dimunition, as discussed in Berndt and Khaled (1979). We will not impose any specific structure on the form of technological change in the analysis that follows. We simply specify, in general terms, the measure of technological change as the negative of the rate of cost dimunition,

$$\lambda = -\frac{\partial \log c}{\partial t}$$

It is possible to analyze changes in cost over time in terms of these measures. Heuristically, it is convenient to use the proportional change in average cost

$$\frac{d \log (c/y)}{dt} = \left(\frac{\partial \log c}{\partial \log y} - 1\right)\frac{d \log y}{dt} + \sum_{i=1}^{M} \frac{\partial \log c}{\partial \log P_i} \, \frac{d \log P_i}{dt} + \frac{\partial \log c}{\partial t}$$

Using Shephard's (1953) lemma to obtain the cost minimizing factor shares,

$$\frac{\partial \log c}{\partial \log P_i} = \frac{P_i X_i}{c} = w_i$$

and the definitions of SCE and λ, we have

$$\frac{d \log(c/y)}{dt} = -\,\text{SCE}\,\frac{d \log y}{dt} + \sum_{i=1}^{M} w_i \, \frac{d \log P_i}{dt} - \lambda$$

Thus, proportional change in average cost is composed, respectively, of the change due to the exploitation of economies of scale, the share-weighted average of the proportional changes in input prices, and the cost dimunition due to technical change.

If technical change is not Hicks neutral, then it may be biased in several ways. Consider the ith factor share,

$$w_i = \frac{\partial \log c}{\partial \log p_i}$$

The change in w_i over time is

$$\frac{dw_i}{dt} = \frac{\partial w_i}{\partial \log y} \frac{d \log y}{dt} + \sum_{j=1}^{M} \frac{\partial w_i}{\partial \log P_j} \frac{d \log p_j}{dt} + \frac{\partial w_i}{\partial t}$$

The change in the ith factor share may also be decomposed into three terms. The first, $(\partial w_i/\partial \log y)(d \log y/dt)$ may be identified with the nonhomotheticity of the production function by noting that

$$\frac{\partial w_i}{\partial \log y} = \partial \left[\frac{(\partial \log c)/(\partial \log p_i)}{\partial \log y} \right]$$

$$= \frac{\partial^2 \log c}{\partial \log p_i \, \partial \log y}$$

$$= \frac{\partial \varepsilon}{\partial \log p_i}$$

the presence of this term allows the factor shares to change over time in the absence of technological change or changes on factor prices. Thus, the first term in dw_i/dt is zero if the production structure is homothetic. We then attribute the first term in dw_i/dt to nonhomotheticity. Define the demand elasticity of the ith factor with respect to the jth price in accordance with Berndt and Christensen (1972) as

$$\eta_{ij} = \sigma_{ij} w_j$$

Routine, though tedious, algebra reveals that the second term in dw_i/dt is

$$\sum_{i=1}^{M} \frac{\partial w_i}{\partial \log p_i} \frac{d \log p_j}{dt}$$

$$= w_i \left[\sum_{i=1}^{M} \eta_{ij} \frac{d \log p_j}{dt} + \left(\frac{d \log p_i}{dt} - \sum_{j=1}^{M} w_j \frac{d \log p_j}{dt} \right) \right]$$

Thus, the second term may be decomposed further into two components, one which clearly reflects the substitution among factors and one which increases or decreases the ith share depending upon whether the increase in the ith factor price is larger or smaller than the share-weighted average of all of the proportional increases in the factor prices. (We will estimate this substitution term in the aggregate rather than isolate its separate components.) We note, in passing, that this result does illuminate an ambiguity in the Allen measure of input substitution. Intuition would suggest that in the absence of changes in scale or technology, the sign of dw_i/dt ought to be determined by that of $\Sigma_{j=1}^{M} \eta_{ij}\, d \log p_j/dt$. We see, though, that this is not the case; the effect, whichever way it goes, can be offset by the second term, $d \log p_i/dt - \Sigma_{j=1}^{M} w_j\, d \log p_j/dt$. Finally, the sign of $\partial w_i/\partial t$ determines whether technical change is biased in the sense of input $i-$ using $(+)$ or input $i-$ saving $(-)$. Stevenson (1980, p. 163) defines a measure of "input bias," I_{bi}, which is, in fact $\partial w_i/\partial t$. We see, however, that this is only one of three influences on relative factor shares over time.

Technical change may also effect economies of scale. In particular, if $\partial \varepsilon/\partial t$ is not zero, then with y and p held constant, the scale properties of average cost will change over time. Obviously, one way to analyze this effect is to examine $\partial \varepsilon/\partial t$ directly. A second way is to consider (for nonhomogeneous production structures only) the change in the location of the output at which average cost is minimized. Let y^* be the scale at which ε equals one. Then $\partial \log y^*/\partial t$ will be of some interest in determining how technical change has effected scale economies.

Stevenson considers the first of these. He defines $TS_c = \partial \varepsilon/\partial t$ as a measure of technological scale bias. However, as shown below, his interpretation of the sign of TS_c as corresponding efficient scale is incorrect. Changes in ε, in fact, relate more closely to changes in the slope of the average cost curve than to changes in its location.

A final characterization of the production structure is offered by the measure of total factor productivity described by Ohta (1974) and Berndt and Khaled (1979). The primal rate of change in total factor productivity is

$$\tau = \partial \log f(\bar{x}, t)/\partial t$$

which can be shown to equal λ/ε.

6.3. Functional Form

Christensen (1977) has proposed a simple modification of the translog cost function (Berndt and Wood, 1975; and Christensen and Greene, 1976) which is flexible enough to allow simultaneous modeling of factor substitution, scale economies, and technical change. In particular, he suggests

$$\log c_t = \alpha_o + \alpha_y \log y + \sum_{i=1}^{M} \alpha_i \log p_i + \alpha_t t$$
$$+ \frac{1}{2}\gamma_{yy}(\log y)^2 + \frac{1}{2}\sum_{j=1}^{M} \gamma_{ij} \log p_i \log p_j$$
$$+ \frac{1}{2}\gamma_{tt}t^2 + \sum_{i=1}^{M} \gamma_{yi} \log y \log p_i + \gamma_{yt} \log y\, t$$
$$+ \sum_{i=1}^{M} \gamma_{ti}\, t \log p_i$$

All of the substitution and scale properties discussed by Christensen and Greene are maintained. In addition, the model is quite general in the types of technical change it will accommodate. Christensen (1977) discusses a number of special cases which amount to simple parametric restrictions.

Although the model is quite flexible, it does imply a restriction on the technology that would be unattractive in view of the results in Christensen and Greene (1976). In particular, the scale parameter is

$$\varepsilon = \frac{\partial \log c}{\partial \log y} = \alpha_y + \gamma_{yy} \log y - \sum_{i=1}^{M} \gamma_{yi} \log p_i + \gamma_{yt} t$$

Solving for the efficient scale, at which average cost reaches its minimum, and ε equals one, we find

$$\log y^* = \frac{1 - \alpha_y - \sum \gamma_{yi} \log p_i - \gamma_{yt} t}{\gamma_{yy}}$$

Differentiating again gives

$$\frac{\partial \log y^*}{\partial t} = -\frac{\gamma_{yt}}{\gamma_{yy}}$$

Thus, the efficient scale grows by a proportional rate $-\gamma_{yt}/\gamma_{yy}$. The evidence already mentioned suggests that in the electric power industry, long-run efficient scale grew rapidly in the 1950s and early 1960s, but very little or not at all in the late 1960s and 1970s. Whether the observed effect can be attributed to rapidly changing relative prices or to a slowdown in technological advance is, of course, an empirical question; but either case is possible and recent trends suggest the latter is more likely. It seems overly restrictive in general to assume constant growth in efficient scale.

Rather than specifically model the particular effects such as the change in efficient scale, we consider a more general specification of the translog cost function in which the time related effects modify the structure of cost nonsystematically. Thus, we specify

$$\log c_t = \alpha_o^t + \sum_{i=1}^{M} \alpha_i^t \log p_{it} + \frac{1}{2} \sum_{i=1}^{M} \sum_{j=1}^{M} \gamma_{ij}^t \log p_{it} \log p_{jt}$$

$$+ \alpha_y^t \log y_t + \frac{1}{2} \gamma_{yy}^t (\log y_t)^2 + \sum_{i=1}^{M} \gamma_{yi}^t \log y_t \log p_{it}$$

where the parameters vary linearly with time according to

$$\alpha_o^t = \alpha_o + \alpha_o' t$$

$$\alpha_i^t = \alpha_i + \alpha_i' t$$

$$\gamma_{ij}^t = \gamma_{ij} + \gamma_{ij}' t$$

$$\alpha_y^t = \alpha_y + \alpha_y' t$$

$$\gamma_{yy}^t = \gamma_{yy} + \gamma_{yy}' t$$

$$\gamma_{yi}^t = \gamma_{yi} + \gamma_{yi}' t$$

This specification allows a non-neutral effect of time on all of the above described characteristics of the production structure.

Stevenson (1980) has proposed the following functional form:

$$\ln c = \alpha_o + \sum \alpha_i \ln p_i + \alpha_y \ln y \cdots + \Phi_o t + \sum \Phi_i t \ln p_i + \Phi_y t \ln y \cdots$$

i.e., a translog cost function augmented by a like function in which all variables are multiplied by time. It is easy to see that these two are, in fact, the same after some rearrangement.

6.4. Estimation

The translog cost function with time varying parameters involves a substantial number of parameters. However, a set of restrictions that must be imposed a priori substantially reduces their number. First, an identifying restriction—symmetry of the second-order terms—is necessary for estimation. Thus, $\gamma_{ij} = \gamma_{ji}$ and $\gamma'_{ij} = \gamma'_{ji}$. Second, linear homogeneity in prices requires the following restrictions:

$$\sum_{i=1}^{M} \alpha_i = 1 \qquad \sum_{i=1}^{M} \alpha'_i = 0$$

$$\sum_{i=1}^{M} \gamma_{yi} = 0 \qquad \sum_{i=1}^{M} \gamma'_{yi} = 0$$

$$\sum_{i=1}^{M} \gamma_{ij} = 0 \qquad = \sum_{i=1}^{M} \gamma_{ji} \; \sum_{i=1}^{M} \gamma'_{ij} = 0 \qquad = \sum_{i=1}^{M} \gamma'_{ji}$$

These restrictions reduce the number of free parameters in the model from $2[(m + 3)(m + 1) - 2m]$ to $(m + 1)(m + 2)$. Even so, the number of free parameters in the model remains large, and estimation will clearly require plentiful data and an efficient estimator.

Direct estimation of the cost function using least squares and time series data is feasible, but is not likely to produce efficient estimates even if a long time series is available. More efficient estimates can be obtained by employing the set of factor share equations given by Shephard's (1953) lemma,[1]

$$w_{it} = \alpha_i^t + \sum_{j=1}^{M} \gamma_{ij}^t \log p_{jt} + \gamma_{yi}^t \log y_t$$

The factor shares provide an additional m estimating equations. We propose estimating jointly, as a multivariate regression model, the cost function and the factor share equations. Since the shares must sum to one at every observation, one is redundant and will be dropped. In order to insure that the estimates are invariant to which equation is omitted, a maximum likelihood estimation procedure is employed. (See Christensen and Greene, 1976, for a discussion of the estimation technique.) Estimates of the parameters of the omitted equation are obtained by using the linear homogeneity restrictions.

We will estimate the parameters of the model using a time series of cross sections. The data consist of observations on 114 firms observed in the 5 years 1955, 1960, 1965, 1970, and 1975. We have modeled the steam generation of electricity as a three-factor process, employing capital (K), labor (L), and fuel (F). Corresponding to the above specification, the set of estimating equations with all restrictions imposed is

$$\log(C_{it}/p_{F_{it}}) = \alpha_o + \alpha_o' t + \Sigma_{j=K,L} (\alpha_j + \alpha_j' t)\log(p_j/p_F)_{it}$$

$$+ \Sigma_{j=K,L} (\gamma_{yi} + \gamma_{yi}' t)\log y_{it} \log(p_j/p_F)_{it}$$

$$+ (\alpha_y + \alpha_y' t)\log y_{it} + \frac{1}{2}(\gamma_{yy} + \gamma_{yy}' t)(\log y_{it})^2$$

$$+ \frac{1}{2}\Sigma_{j=K,L} (\gamma_{jj} + \gamma_{jj}' t)[\log(p_j/p_F)_{it}]^2$$

$$+ (\gamma_{KL} + \gamma_{KL}' t)\log(p_K/p_F)_{it} \log(p_L/p_F)_{it} + \varepsilon_{C_{it}}$$

$$w_{K_{it}} = \alpha_K + \alpha_K' t + \overset{L}{\Sigma}_{j=K,L} (\gamma_{Kj} + \gamma_{Kj}' t)\log(p_j/p_F)_{it}$$

$$+ (\gamma_{yK} + \gamma_{yK}' t)\log y + \varepsilon_{K_{it}}$$

$$w_{L_{it}} = (\alpha_L + \alpha_L' t) + \Sigma_{j=K,L} (\gamma_{jL} + \gamma_{jL}' t)\log(p_j/p_F)_{it}$$

$$+ (\gamma_{yL} + \gamma_{yL}' t)\log y + \varepsilon_{L_{it}}$$

$$w_{F_{it}} = 1 - w_{K_{it}} - w_{L_{it}}$$

where ε_c, ε_K, and ε_L are random disturbances with zero means.

There are numerous stochastic specifications possible, each of which implies a particular estimation technique. Let $\bar{\varepsilon}_{it}' = (\varepsilon_{c_{it}}, \varepsilon_{K_{it}}, \varepsilon_{L_{it}})$. Since the cross-sectional units are independent, $E(\bar{\varepsilon}_{it}\bar{\varepsilon}_{it}\bar{\varepsilon}_{js}') = 0$ for all $i \neq j$ whether or not $t = s$. The most general specification would then be $E(\bar{\varepsilon}_{it}\bar{\varepsilon}_{is}') = \Omega_{ts}$, a 3×3 matrix, which allows for intercorrelation among the three disturbances in $\bar{\varepsilon}_{it}$ and correlation across time. If the observations are stacked in $N = 114$ sets of 5 trivariate observations, and if Ω is the 15×15 positive definite matrix each of whose 25 3×3 blocks is Ω_{ts}, then the covariance for the full set of observations is $\Omega \times I_{114}$. The model can be estimated in this form by a logical extension of the multivariate regression model described above. An alternative, which, although more restrictive, is computationally more burdensome, is the multivariate error components model analyzed by Avery (1977). Most of the estimates discussed below are based upon the further restriction $\Omega_{ts} = 0$ if $t \neq s$ and $\Omega_{tt} = \Omega_{ss}$ for all t and s. This last restriction reduces the set of estimating equations to a standard three-equation multivariate regression model which will be estimated using a total of 5×114 or 570 observations. Since the time separation between observations is so long (five years) the assumption of zero correlation across time seems reasonable. This formulation results in the same estimator used by Stevenson (1980). Note, since he used only two time periods, coding $t = 0$, 1, his technique amounts to estimating separate equations for two years while constraining $\Omega_{11} = \Omega_{22}$ and $\Omega_{12} = 0$.

6.5. Data

As indicated, the data used for this study are a time series of cross sections. The 114 firms analyzed are essentially the same sample used in the earlier Christensen and Greene (1976) paper. Ten smaller firms have been omitted because of a lack of sufficient available data.

Total costs are the sum of capital, labor, and fuel expenditure used in steam generation only.[2] Input prices for the three inputs are an index number reflecting the costs of borrowing and construction, dollars per man-year, and cents per million BTU respectively. Output is measured in millions by kilowatt hours per year. Further details on the construction of these variables may be found in Christensen and Greene (1976).

Finally, for convenience, the time variable is coded $-2, -1, 0, 1$, and 2 corresponding respectively to 1955, 1960, 1965, 1970, and 1975.

6.6. Empirical Results

Parameter Estimates. Table 6–1 presents the maximum likelihood estimates of the 30 restricted parameters of the cost function. These estimates can, in turn, be used to derive yearly specific-parameter estimates, which are computed directly using $\alpha_i^t = \alpha_i + \alpha_i' t$ and $\gamma_{ij}^t = \gamma_{ij} + \gamma_{ij}' t$ as defined above.

Table 6–1. Cost Function Parameter Estimates (asymptotic *t* ratios in parentheses)

α_o	−7.522	(−47.48)	α'_o	−0.112	(−1.23)
α_K	0.001	(0.02)	α'_K	0.110	(4.05)
α_L	0.209	(3.91)	α'_L	−0.118	(−3.81)
α_F	0.790	(23.09)	α'_F	0.008	(0.35)
α_y	0.567	(20.33)	α'_y	0.060	(3.66)
γ_{KK}	0.036	(2.87)	γ'_{KK}	0.042	(5.97)
γ_{LL}	−0.005	(−0.43)	γ'_{LL}	0.033	(4.87)
γ_{FF}	0.134	(16.50)	γ'_{FF}	−0.013	(−2.46)
γ_{KL}	0.051	(4.92)	γ'_{KL}	−0.044	(−7.66)
γ_{KF}	−0.088	(−10.78)	γ'_{KF}	0.002	(0.38)
γ_{LF}	−0.046	(−7.29)	γ'_{LF}	0.011	(2.86)
γ_{yy}	0.049	(12.66)	γ'_{yy}	−0.005	(−2.13)
γ_{yK}	−0.010	(−4.39)	γ'_{yK}	0.002	(1.30)
γ_{yL}	−0.011	(−7.26)	γ'_{yL}	−0.0025	(−2.32)
γ_{yF}	0.021	(9.48)	γ'_{yF}	0.0005	(0.32)

Numerous restrictions can be placed on the structure of production (e.g., homotheticity) and on the nature of the technical change (e.g., Hicks-neutral) by using simple restrictions on the parameters (see Christensen and Greene, 1976.) However, the likelihood ratio tests of these hypotheses lead to rejection at any reasonable level of significance. Thus, the results discussed below are based on the specification in Table 6–1.

The Structure of Cost and Production Over Time. As discussed above, the observed changes in average cost can be attributed to three effects, the exhaustion of scale economies, nominal changes in input prices, and cost reducing technological change.

6.7. Scale Effects

One clear effect has been a movement of the "efficient scale" of production, i.e., the level of output at which average cost is minimized. In the earlier years, the size of the largest available generating units grew substantially, to a maximum of about 1300 megawatts. At the same time, firms were, through pooling arrangements, taking advantages of economies of shared reserve capacity. (See Christensen and Greene, 1976.) Apparently, however, the rapid growth of efficient scale tapered off in the late 1960s, and stopped altogether in the 1970s. The estimated values of the efficient scale are shown in Table 6–2.

Most firms in the industry were, in each year, substantially smaller than the scales in Table 6–2, and thus had considerable economies of scale available to them. At the same time, the growth of most firms was quite rapid, in fact faster than that of the efficient scale. The net effects can be seen in Table 6–3. In general, since firms were growing faster than the minimum efficient scale, scale economies were, in fact, being exhausted. The result can be seen in each column of Table 6–3, in which it is shown that the firm at each percentile exhibits reduced scale economies in succeeding years. (Note that the median firm in 1960 is different from that in 1955. The same effect is observed, however, if the 1955 median firm is followed through the succeeding years.)

The growth of firms and the growth of the minimum efficient scale can be considered simultaneously by examining the number of firms, and the contribution of these firms to total output, that operate under conditions we estimate to be of constant returns to scale. Table 6–4 lists the yearly partitioning of the sample into those firms that exhibit statistically significant (by a one-sided t test) economies of scale (i.e., SCE greater than zero) and those that do not. The number of firms that exhibit constant returns to scale increases rapidly, as does the proportion of output produced under constant returns to scale. By 1975, nearly 60% of the output in the sample (which is nearly 80% of industry output) is produced under essentially constant cost conditions. (Note, the substantially reduced lower bound of the constant cost region for 1975 reflects a relatively flat estimated cost curve for this year.)

The behavior of the minimum efficient scale and the downward movement of the lower bound of the constant cost region suggest that in addition to shifting vertically from year to year, the average cost curve has changed shape, and in particular has become flatter in the later years. One way to examine this effect analytically is to fix output, and to examine the changes in SCE. In particular, $\partial \text{SCE}/\partial t$ is indicative of the changing shape of average cost. From the above definition,

$$\frac{\partial \text{SCE}}{\partial t} = -(\alpha'_y + \gamma'_{yy} \log y + \sum_{i=1}^{M} \gamma'_{yi} \log p_i$$

Table 6–5 lists values of $\partial \text{SCE}/\partial t$ for several values of y, for each year. Negative values of the derivative below the efficient scale and positive values above the efficient scale imply reduction in the slope of the cost curve. In general, these results imply that the average cost curve becomes flatter throughout the period.

Table 6–2. Estimates of Efficient Scale (in million KWH)

	1955		*1960*		*1965*		*1970*		*1975*
KWH	21,229		24,698		26,000		33,200		33,619
Average yearly growth		3.07%		1.03%		5.01%		0.25%	

Table 6–3. Scale Economies by Quartiles of Output

		25%	*50%*	*75%*	*Sample Mean*
1955	Output	566	1787	3794	3021
	SCE	0.216	0.147	0.102	0.116
	(*t* ratio)	(22.63)	(12.63)	(6.87)	(8.38)
1960	Output	780	2598	5369	4317
	SCE	0.188	0.123	0.083	0.095
	(*t* ratio)	(24.25)	(12.28)	(6.69)	(8.15)
1965	Output	1447	3733	7955	6200
	SCE	0.144	0.097	0.060	0.072
	(*t* ratio)	(20.75)	(11.28)	(5.58)	(7.23)
1970	Output	2258	5708	12542	9336
	SCE	0.120	0.078	0.043	0.056
	(*t* ratio)	(14.39)	(7.58)	(3.37)	(4.76)
1975	Output	2018	7018	13850	10242
	SCE	0.096	0.046	0.020	0.031
	(*t* ratio)	(9.51)	(3.29)	(1.13)	(1.99)

Table 6–4. Significant Scale Economies

	Lower Bound of Region with No Significant Economies	*Number of Firms Above Lower Bound (Total = 114)*	*Proportion of Output*
1955	10,400	6	26.3%
1960	13,100	8	32.4%
1965	17,400	9	34.2%
1970	17,300	16	45.6%
1975	12,100	24	57.8%

Table 6–5. Estimated Values of $\partial SCE/\partial t$

Output (million KWH)	*Year*				
	1955	*1960*	*1965*	*1970*	*1975*
1,000	−0.0144	−0.0448	−0.0143	−0.0133	−0.0125
5,000	−0.0063	−0.0067	−0.0062	−0.0052	−0.0044
10,000	−0.0028	−0.0032	−0.0029	−0.0017	−0.0009
15,000	−0.0008	−0.0012	−0.0007	0.0003	0.0011
25,000	0.0017	0.0013	0.0018	0.0028	0.0036
35,000	0.0034	0.0030	0.0035	0.0045	0.0053
Efficient scale	21,229	24,698	26,000	33,200	33,619

Combining all of these effects, the reduced growth in efficient scale, the continued growth of the firms in the sample, and the flattening of the average cost curves, we conclude that a growing proportion of output is being and will be produced under constant cost conditions. Moreover, it seems likely that the effects of technological change on economies of scale are being greatly diminished. Further technical change will likely be neutral with respect to scale (i.e., will be reflected in proportional vertical displacement of the cost curve).

6.8. Changing Input Prices

It is clear that considerable movement of the average cost of production has been brought about by changes in the nominal prices of the inputs. At the same time, as shown in Table 6–6, relative prices have also changed considerably. For the first 18 years of the period examined here, the price of fuel relative to capital and labor declined steadily. As an apparent consequence, there was a steady trend toward construction of larger, more fuel intensive units. Although the relative price of fuel rose dramatically in 1973, it is not clear whether, in relative terms, this was a one time change or not. Fuel prices have continued to rise, but construction and capital costs have, since 1973, risen at least as rapidly.

Demand elasticities and elasticities of substitution for the five years are displayed in Table 6–7. Two figures in the table are noteworthy. First, the own-price elasticity of demand for fuel is extremely small, and declining. Second, the elasticity of substitution between capital and fuel is also quite small. The net effect is that the anticipated very rapid increases in the costs of

Table 6–6. Relative Prices at Sample Means

	Capital/Fuel	*Labor/Fuel*
1955	1.78	157
1960	2.85	190
1965	2.90	234
1970	6.13	264
1975	3.34	114

conventional fossil fuels will translate almost undiminished into higher total costs as the cost share of fuel rises in response. The results also suggest very little opportunity for the substitution of fuel-saving, capital-intensive hardware for present units.

Considerable adjustment has also occurred in the factor cost shares. The fitted cost shares, and the year-to-year changes are shown in Table 6–8. As discussed above, this adjustment can be decomposed into three components, due to nonhomotheticity of the production process, factor substitution, and technological change. An analysis of these changes is displayed in Table 6–9. Because of the long span between years, and the changing values of the shares and elasticities, in decomposing the change in the factor shares, the average of the beginning- and end-year share weights and elasticities is used.

Table 6–7. Estimated Demand Elasticities and Elasticities of Substitution at Mean Values of Prices and Output

	Own-Price Elasticities				
	1955	*1960*	*1965*	*1970*	*1975*
Capital	−0.721	−0.788	−0.604	−0.326	−0.412
Labor	−1.630	−1.024	−0.929	−0.664	−0.175
Fuel	−0.180	−0.168	−0.157	−0.145	−0.069

	Elasticities of Substitution				
	1955	*1960*	*1965*	*1970*	*1975*
Capital-fuel	0.545	0.350	0.452	0.386	0.192
Capital-labor	4.560	3.181	2.748	1.215	2.164
Fuel-labor	−0.233	0.461	0.711	1.373	0.627

Table 6–8. Cost Shares at Mean Prices and Output and Year-to-Year Changes

	Capital		*Labor*		*Fuel*	
	Fitted	*Observed*	*Fitted*	*Observed*	*Fitted*	*Observed*
1955	0.3384	0.400	0.0796	0.098	0.5820	0.502
(change)	(−0.0179)	(−0.162)	(0.0722)	(0.086)	(−0.0543)	(0.076)
1960	0.3205	0.238	0.1518	0.184	0.5277	0.578
(change)	(−0.0854)	(0.015)	(−0.0199)	(−0.068)	(0.0973)	(0.053)
1965	0.2351	0.253	0.1399	0.116	0.6250	0.631
(change)	(−0.0191)	(−0.031)	(−0.0011)	(−0.033)	(0.0180)	(−0.002)
1970	0.2160	0.222	0.1410	0.149	0.6430	0.629
(change)	(−0.0786)	(−0.079)	(−0.0621)	(−0.067)	(0.1407)	(0.146)
1975	0.1374	0.143	0.0789	0.082	0.7837	0.775

Table 6–9. Decomposition of Year-to-Year Changes in Factor Cost Shares

Source of Adjustment	*1955–1960*	*1960–1965*	*1965–1970*	*1970–1975*
Nonhomotheticity				
K	−0.0056	−0.0048	−0.0046	−0.0007
L	−0.0034	−0.0044	−0.0061	−0.0014
F	0.0090	0.0092	0.0107	0.0021
Substitution				
K	0.0037	0.0183	0.0973	−0.0365
L	0.0606	−0.0040	0.0496	−0.0431
F	−0.0643	−0.0143	−0.1469	0.0796
Biased technological change				
K	−0.0747	−0.0723	−0.0535	−0.0342
L	0.0091	0.0043	−0.0136	−0.0291
F	0.0656	0.0680	0.0671	0.0633
Total				
K	−0.0766	−0.0588	0.0392	−0.0714
L	0.0663	−0.0041	0.0299	−0.0737
F	0.0103	0.0629	−0.0691	0.1450

In general, the nonhomotheticity and biased technological change tend to be reinforcing. Both tend to increase the cost share of fuel and decrease those of labor and capital. Of these two effects, the nonhomotheticity is the smaller, leading only to very minor adjustments in the cost shares. The effect of technical change is pronounced, and suggests considerable shifting of costs in the direction of fuel-using equipment.

6.9. Technological Change

Much of the technological change in conventional fossil-fueled electricity generation has involved the design of larger units employing higher temperature and higher pressure boilers. As shown above, these changes have tended to be fuel intensive; the average cost share for fuel has increased from about 60% to about 80%, although three quarters of the increase occurred after 1970. Throughout the period, technological change resulted in a large and steady reduction in average cost. After accounting for the effects of price changes and the exploitation of economies of scale, we find that costs of production fell an average of more than 2.5% per year as a result of technological change. Berndt and Khaled (1979) obtain a comparable figure for the entire U.S. manufacturing sector of roughly 0.75% per year. The values of λ computed from the estimated average cost function are shown in Table 6–10.

These values are substantially higher than those presented by Stevenson (1980, see p. 172). His estimate of 1.5 to 1.7% per year is roughly half of that found here. Since the models used are the same, this must be due in large measure to differences in the data sets. A cursory look at our respective parameter estimates reveals generally large differences.

As suggested by Ohta (1974), we can measure the effect of technological change on productivity indirectly using $\tau = \lambda/(1 - \text{SCE})$. The values of τ in Table 6–11 suggest productivity increases on the order of 3% per year, again a surprisingly high rate of change. The productivity increase can be partially decomposed by examining the behavior of the input-output ratios. Using Shephard's lemma, we find

$$\frac{\partial \ln x_i/y}{\partial t} = -\lambda + \frac{\partial \log w_i}{\partial t}$$

$$= -\lambda + \frac{1}{w_i}\frac{\partial w_i}{\partial t} \qquad i = K, L, F$$

Values for these derivatives are displayed in Table 6–12. In spite of the rapid increase in the price of fuel and in its cost share, we find that the fuel output ratio declines over most of the period. The greatest yearly decline occurs in the period 1965 to 1970. An examination of industry sources, e.g., FPC (1965–1975), shows that system heat rates (BTU/KWH) have, indeed, declined over most of the period examined here, although the largest declines seem to have occurred well before 1975.

Table 6–10. Cost Reductions Due to Technical Change

Year	*1955*	*1960*	*1965*	*1970*	*1975*
λ	−0.1123	−0.1417	−0.1419	−0.1839	−0.1314
Implied estimated yearly cost reduction	2.35%	3.01%	3.01%	3.98%	2.78%

Table 6–11. Estimated Rates of Change of Factor Productivity

Year	*1955*		*1960*		*1965*		*1970*		*1975*
τ	0.1271		0.1566		0.1530		0.1949		0.1357
Average yearly change in factor productivity	2.84	2.69% 2.84		2.92% 3.10		3.26% 3.48		3.11% 3.31	

Table 6–12. Estimated Yearly Rates of Change in Input-Output Ratios

	1955	*1960*	*1965*	*1970*	*1975*
Capital/Output	−7.5%	−9.2%	10.5%	8.8%	−7.9%
Labor/Output	−0.4%	−1.5%	−3.4%	−8.6%	−14.8%
Fuel/Output	0.1%	−0.3%	−0.5%	−1.3%	−0.9%

6.10. Summary and Conclusions

We have found three effects contributing to the changes in average cost. These effects are summarized in Table 6–13. The results are striking. First, as suggested in our earlier paper (Christensen and Greene, 1976), economies of scale are becoming less and less important at the firm level. The cost reductions due to the exploitation of economies of scale for the average firm decline throughout the 1955–1975 period, and are almost negligible from 1970 to 1975. Even extrapolating the 1970–1975 cost reduction figure to the 1965–1970 rate of output growth produces cost reduction of only 2.24%, 69% of the comparable 1965–1970 figure. Second, the rate of technological change in the electric power industry has been dramatic, resulting in cost savings of well over 2.5% per year and in substantial declines in the fuel output and capital output ratios.

Notes

1. The propriety of the underlying assumption of cost minimization is argued in Christensen and Greene (1976). In essence, with mandated rates, regulated electric utilities must satisfy all demand forthcoming at minimum cost.

Table 6–13. Summary of Decomposition of Changes in Average Generation Costs, 1955–1975 (in average yearly rates of change over the period)

Period	*Exploitation of Scale Economies*	*Technological Change*	*Input Price Changes*	*Total*
1955–1960	−0.92%	−2.68%	5.48%	1.88%
1960–1965	−0.74%	−3.01%	0.25%	−3.50%
1965–1970	−0.66%	−3.48%	7.93%	3.79%
1970–1975	−0.09%	−3.37%	23.78%	20.32%

2. The firms all employ conventional steam generators for at least 90% of their output. Costs are allocated to thermal generation on the basis of the proportion of thermal steam generation relative to total when the proportion is less than 100%.

References

Avery, R., 1977, "Error Components and Seemingly Unrelated Regressions," *Econometria* 45:199–213.

Berndt, E., and L. R. Christensen, 1972, "The Translog Function and the Substitution of Equipment Structures and Labor in U.S. Manufacturing, 1947–1971," The Journal of Econometrics, vol 1, no. 1.

Berndt, E., and M. Khaled, 1979, "Parametric Productivity Measurement and Choice Among Flexible Functional Forms," *Journal of Political Economy* 87, no. 6:1220–1245.

Berndt, E., and D. Wood, 1975, "Technology, Prices, and the Derived Demand for Energy," *Review of Economics and Statistics* 57:259–268.

Christensen, L. R., 1977, "Simultaneous Estimation of Technical Change and Scale Economies," Unpublished Memorandum, Department of Economics, University of Wisconsin, March 1977.

Christensen, L., and W. Greene, 1976, "Economies of Scale in U.S. Electric Power Generation," *Journal of Political Economy* 84, 4 (pt. 1):655–676.

Diamond, P.; D. McFadden; and M. Rodriguez, 1978, "Measurement of the Elasticity of Factor Substitution and Bias of Technical Change," in M. Fuss and D. McFadden, eds., *Production Economics: A Dual Approach to Theory and Application, vol. 2* (Amsterdam: North Holland).

Federal Power Commission, *Statistics of Privately Owned Electric Utilities in the United States, Classes A and B* Annual Supplements (Washington, D.C.: U.S. Government Printing Office).

Førsund, F., and L. Hjalmarsson, 1979, "Frontier Production Functions and Technical Progress," *Econometrica* 47, no. 4:883–900.

Hanoch, G., 1975, "The Elasticity of Scale and the Shape of Average Costs," *American Economic Review* 65, no. 3:492–497.

Ohta, M., 1974, "A Note on the Duality Between Production and Cost Functions: Returns to Scale and the Rate of Technological Progress," *Economic Studies Quarterly* 25:63–65.

Sato, R., 1970, "The Estimation of Biased Technical Progress and the Production Function," *International Economic Review* 11:179–208.

Sato, R., and P. Calem, "Lie Group Methods and the Theory of Estimating Total Productivity," chapter 7 of this volume.

Shephard, R. W., 1953, *Cost and Production Functions* (Princeton, N.J.: Princeton University Press).

Stevenson, R., 1980, "Measuring Technological Bias," *American Economic Review* 70, no. 1:162–173.

Woodward, G. T., "A Factor Augmenting Approach for Studying Capital Measurement, Obsolescence, and the Recent Productivity Slowdown," chapter 5 of this volume.

7 LIE GROUP METHODS AND THE THEORY OF ESTIMATING TOTAL PRODUCTIVITY

R. Sato and P. S. Calem

7.1. Introduction and Summary

In the existing literature, one finds that there are two approaches to estimating technical progress. The *traditional approach* or the *primal approach* employs a linear homogeneous production function and measures technical progress in terms of contributions to growth in output that are not attributable to increases in inputs. The works of Kendrick and Sato (1963), Sato (1970), Binswanger (1974), and Denny and May (1979) can be placed in the category of the traditional approach to measuring technical progress.

An alternative approach, the *dual approach*, postulates the existence of an aggregate cost function, assumes a functional form for this cost function (usually translog), and measures technical progress in terms of the contributions to changes in cost not attributable to changes in the prices of inputs. This approach was taken by Christensen and Greene (1976). They utilized a translog cost function to estimate returns to scale and the rate of technical progress in the Electric Power Industry. Berndt and Khaled (1979) also take

The authors acknowledge useful comments by Dale Jorgenson, Rolf Färe, and A. Dogramaci.

this approach. They assume a more general functional form for their cost function in order to measure the rate of technical progress in U.S. manufacturing. Most recently, Greene (1982) takes the dual approach. He uses a sophisticated version of the translog cost function to estimate scale economies, factor substitution, and rates of technical progress, which are allowed to vary over time. The dual approach is also used by Woodward (1982).

This paper is about theoretical developments within the traditional framework for estimating productivity. It is possible to derive corresponding results within the dual framework. In particular, this paper discusses some applications of Lie group methods to the theory of measuring productivity.

The methods of Lie group theory (see Sato, 1980 and 1981) can be applied in several illuminating ways to the theory of productivity estimation. One such application is to the question of whether or not technical progress may be estimated independently of returns to scale. The main theoretical result is that only in certain cases is technical progress necessarily indistinguishable from a scale effect. In section 7.2, we review the development of this result. In section 7.3, we review the method of Kendrick and Sato (1963) for estimating technical progress, and we generalize the Sato (1970) method to the case of $n \geq 2$ factors of production. In section 7.4, we show that the Kendrick-Sato method cannot be used to separately estimate technical progress and a scale effect. We also show how the Sato (1970) method can be extended to allow separate estimation of technical progress and a scale effect.

Lie group theory also provides a new tool for estimating the parameters of a technical progress transformation. This is discussed in section 7.5. In section 7.6, we show how a given production relationship may be interpreted as the result of a Lie transformation on another production function. Several examples are presented and some possible applications are stated.

7.2. Holotheticity and the Scale Effect: Lie Group Theory

Lie group theory and the concept of *holotheticity* provide the key to resolving what has become known as the "Solow-Stigler controversy." The controversy centers around the question of whether or not it is possible in empirical estimations to distinguish increasing returns to scale effects from technical progress.

The existing techniques that apply the traditional approach to estimating technical progress assume a constant returns to scale production function.

An existing technique will be called "admissible" if it can be modified in a way that allows estimation of both technical progress and increasing returns to scale effects. Sato (1980, 1981), utilizing Lie group theory and the concept of holotheticity, shows that only certain existing techniques are not admissible. Thus, the Solow-Stigler controversy is reduced to the problem of reformulating an admissible procedure so as to allow independent estimation of technical progress and scale effects.

The issue of measuring the role of technical progress in economic growth has received the attention of economists for a number of years. In their survey article, "The Theory of Economic Growth," Hahn and Matthews (1964, pp. 832) write:

> Much empirical work in the 1950s was inspired by the simple type of approach to technical progress we have been discussing. The basic procedure is to estimate the contributions made to the growth in output by increases in the inputs of labor and capital over a period, and to deduct the result from the overall growth in output. The remainder is attributed to technical progress. In the past, these estimations involved production functions that were linear homogeneous and the results were almost always to show that technical progress contributes much more to growth than does capital accumulation. Policy conclusions were drawn to the effect that national policies of belt tightening were unlikely to be worthwhile.

Stigler (1961) criticized the validity of estimations of technical progress that assume linear homogenous production functions. He argued on economic grounds that we should reject the linear homogeneous production function in favor of one that allows increasing returns to scale. He observed that as an economy grows in size it becomes more efficient, due to increased specialization of the labor force, introduction of industries with "sharply defined functions" that enhance the overall productivity of the business sector, etc. He concluded that it is essential to the theory of economic growth to distinguish between the contributions of increasing returns to scale and the contributions of technical progress to growth and to measure the respective magnitudes of each.

Solow (1961), though agreeing in principle with Stigler, expressed scepticism as to whether the separate measurement of scale effects and technical progress effects could be accomplished. Sato (1980, 1981) shows that in special cases it *will* be impossible to distinguish scale effects from technical progress. In general, it will not be impossible. Whether or not it will be possible depends upon the forms of the technological progress transformation and production function we assume. For instance, suppose $Y = F(f(K, L))$ is a homothetic production function and technical progress is of the uniform factor-augmenting type.

$$\bar{K} = T(t)K$$
$$\bar{L} = T(t)L$$

Then, after introducing technical progress into the production function we have

$$\begin{aligned} Y = F[f(\bar{K}, \bar{L})] &= F[f(T(t)K, T(t)L] \\ &= F[T(t)f(K, L)] \\ &= G_t[f(K L)]. \end{aligned}$$

But this is exactly what a scale effect would be. In this case, the impact of the technological change is indistinguishable from a scale effect. Such a pathological circumstance can be considered the source of the Solow-Stigler controversy.

We make the following definition (Sato, 1980, 1981):

> When the impact of technical progress on the production function is transformed to a scale effect, leaving the isoquants invariant, then the production function is said to be *holothetic* under the given type of technical progress.

Thus, in order to empirically identify both the scale and technical progress effects, the production function must not be holothetic under the given type of technical progress. We have defined what it is we must avoid. To know how to avoid it is the key to resolving the Solow-Stigler controversy. Sato (1980, 1981) establishes the criterion by which we can know that a production function will be holothetic under a given technological progress transformation. It is worth summarizing the development of this result.

Consider a production function $f(K, L)$ with the usual properties (twice continuously differentiable, etc.). Assume that when exogenous technical progress is introduced, it can be expressed as "effective capital" and "effective labor," leaving the form of the production function unchanged; i.e., $f(K, L, t) = f(\bar{K}, \bar{L})$, where the technical progress transformation is T: $\bar{K} = \Phi(K, L, t)$, $\bar{L} = \psi(K, L, t)$. We can formalize the notion of holotheticity as follows:

f is holothetic under T if and only if

$$Y = f[\Phi(K, L, t), \psi(K, L, t)] = F_t[f(K, L)]$$

Equivalently, f is holothetic under T if and only if

$$Y = f(K, L, t) = g[h(K, L), t]$$

where $h(K, L) = f(K, L, O)$. There are two equivalent interpretations of holotheticity:

1. The impact of technical progress is completely absorbed as a scale effect.
2. The isoquant map is not affected by the given type of technical progress.

The Figure 7–1 illustrates how holothetic technical progress is indistinguishable from a scale effect. The isoquants of the function $F[f(K, L)]$ coincide with the isoquants of $F_t[f(K, L)] = f(K, L, t)$.

Assuming that the technical progress transformations Φ and ψ have the Lie group properties will enable us to apply Lie Group Theory to the study of holotheticity. These properties are:

Property 1: The successive performance of two transformations t and $\bar{t}$ is representable as a single transformation, denoted $t + \bar{t}$; i.e.,

$$\Phi[\Phi(K, L, t), \psi(K, L, t), \bar{t}] = \Phi(K, L, t + \bar{t})$$

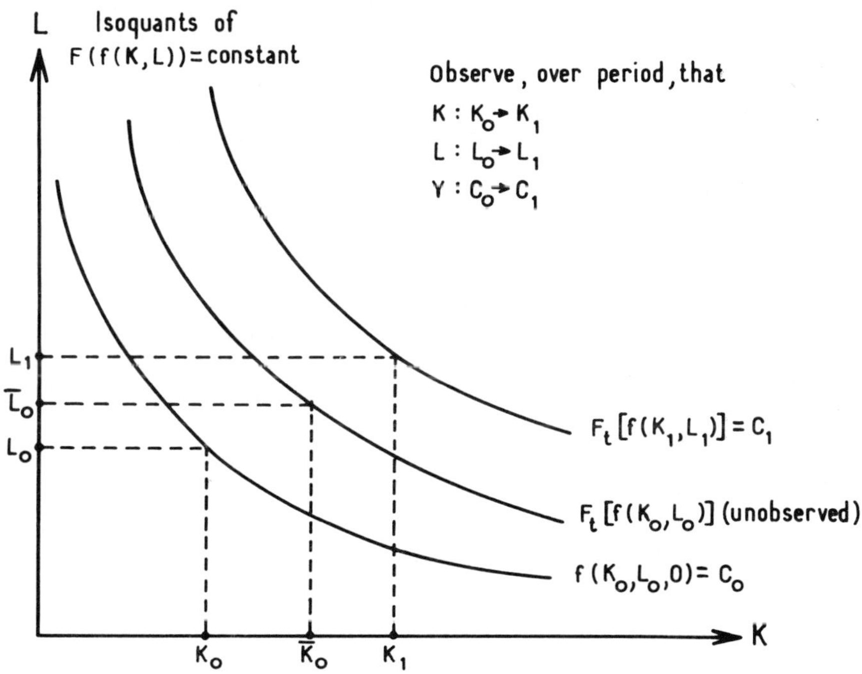

Figure 7–1.

and

$$\psi[\Phi(K, L, t), \psi(K, L, t), \bar{t}\,] = \psi(K, L, t + \bar{t}\,)$$

Property 2: $t = 0$ gives the identity transformation T_o:

$$\Phi(K, L, 0) = K \qquad \text{and} \qquad \psi(K, L, 0) = L$$

Property 3: For any transformation T_t there exists an inverse transformation T_t^{-1} so that $T_t^{-1} \cdot T_t = T_0 = T_t \cdot T_t^{-1}$. The inverse transformation is represented by $-t$; i.e.,

$$\Phi[\Phi(K, L, t), \psi(K, L, t), -t] = K$$

and

$$\psi[\Phi(K, L, t), \psi(K, L, t), -t] = L$$

We make the following definition:

Suppose the transformations $\Phi(K, L, t)$ and $\psi(K, L, t)$ form a Lie transformation group T (i.e., satisfy properties 1–3). A family of curves $f(K, L) = c$ is said to be invariant under T if every transformation of the group transforms each curve of the family into some curve of the family; i.e., $f(\Phi(K, L, t), \psi(K, L, t)] = F_t[f(K, L)]$ for all t.

It is obvious that holotheticity of the production function f under the technical progress transformation T is a special case of invariance of a family of curves under a group; the invariant curves are the isoquants of f.

The fundamental result (Sato, 1980, 1981) is this:

Theorem: Suppose the technical progress transformations T: $\bar{K} = \Phi(K, L, t), \bar{L} = \psi(K, L, t)$ satisfy the Lie group properties. Then $f(K, L)$ is holothetic under T if and only if $f(K, L)$ satisfies:

$$(*) \quad \left[\frac{\partial \Phi}{\partial t}\Big|_{t=0}\right] \frac{\partial f}{\partial K} + \left[\frac{\partial \psi}{\partial t}\Big|_{t=0}\right] \frac{\partial f}{\partial L} = G(f) \qquad (G \neq 0 \text{ is arbitrary})$$

This theorem follows from a result of Lie group theory which states that a family of curves $f(K, L) = c$ is invariant under the group T is and only if $f(K, L)$ is a solution to the partial differential equation (*). This is an equation of the form

$$\xi(K, L) \frac{\partial f}{\partial K} + \eta(K, L) \frac{\partial f}{\partial L} = G(f)$$

which is known to have a unique general solution.

This theorem provides the key to resolving the Solow-Stigler controversy. There will be no confusion of scale effect and technical progress effect so long as the production function does not belong to the family that is holothetic under the assumed type of technical progress. The necessary and sufficient condition for holotheticity is that the production function satisfy the p.d.e. (*). This result can be illustrated by the following examples:

Example A: Suppose technical progress is the uniform (neutral) factor augmenting type:

$$T: \quad \bar{K} = e^{\gamma t}K; \ \bar{L} = e^{\gamma t}L$$

It is easily verified that these transformations form a Lie group. The p.d.e. defining the holothetic technology is

$$\gamma K \frac{\partial f}{\partial K} + \gamma L \frac{\partial f}{\partial L} = G(f)$$

The solution is the class of homothetic production functions; i.e., functions of the form $Y = g[f(K, L)]$ where $f(K, L)$ is homogeneous degree one. Thus, in order to be able to estimate the uniform technical progress and scale effect, we cannot assume the homothetic technology.

Example B: Suppose technical progress T is the nonuniform, biased type: $\bar{K} = e^{\gamma_1 t}K$, $\bar{L} = e^{\gamma_2 t}L$. Again, it is easily verified that these transformations form a Lie group. The p.d.e.

$$\gamma_1 K \frac{\partial f}{\partial K} + \gamma_2 L \frac{\partial f}{\partial L} = G(f)$$

defines the holothetic technology. The solution is the family of "almost homothetic" functions

$$Y = f\left[K^{1/\gamma_1} Q\left(\frac{L^{\gamma_2}}{K^{\gamma_1}}\right)\right]$$

Again, we must use some other family to isolate scale effect from technical progress effect.

7.3. Estimation Procedures

Sato's result can be applied to choosing admissible estimation procedures. To understand how this is accomplished, it is necessary to first examine some procedures for estimating technical progress that employ a linear homogeneous production function (constant returns to scale). The methods to be examined are the Kendrick-Sato (1963) method and a multifactor generalization of the Sato (1970) method. The basic assumptions of the Kendrick-Sato method are:

Assumption 1: Hicks-neutral technical progress and a linear homogeneous production function; i.e., $Y(t) = T(t)F(K, L)$, $T(t) > 1$.

Assumption 2: The marginal productivities of capital and labor are approximately equal to the rate of return on capital and the wage rate, respectively; i.e., $\pi = \partial F/\partial K$ and $w = \partial F/\partial L$, where π is the rate of return on capital and w is the wage rate.

By assumption 2 we have $Y/f(K, L) = T(t)$, from which it follows that:

$$\frac{\dot{T}}{T} = \frac{\dot{Y}}{Y} - \left[\frac{\partial Y}{\partial K}\frac{\dot{K}}{K}\frac{K}{Y} + \frac{\partial Y}{\partial L}\frac{\dot{L}}{L}\frac{L}{Y}\right]$$

Hence,

$$\frac{\dot{T}}{T} = \frac{\dot{Y}}{Y} - \left[\alpha\frac{\dot{K}}{K} + \beta\frac{\dot{L}}{L}\right] \tag{7–1}$$

where $\alpha = \pi K/Y$ and $\beta = wL/Y$.

Equation (7–1) can be used to estimate $\dot{T}/T$. Moreover, the following procedure makes it possible to estimate the production function $T(t)f(K, L)$:

1. Specify $T(t) = A_0 e^{(\dot{T}/T)t}$
2. Specify the elasticity of substitution to be constant, and in particular, specify the family of production functions to be of the form $Y = [T(t)KL]/(aL^\theta + bK^\theta)^{1/\theta}$.
3. Estimate the elasticity of substitution $\sigma = (\dot{K}/K - \dot{L}/L)/(\dot{w}/w - \dot{\pi}/\pi)$.

We will construct a multifactor generalization of the Sato (1970) method. We assume:

Assumption 3: Non-neutral factor augmenting technical progress and a linear homogeneous production function

$$Y = F[A_1(t)X_1(t), \ldots, A_n(t)X_n(t)]$$

Assumption 4: The real return to factor $i = w_i = \partial F/\partial X_i$, $i = 1, \ldots, n$.

Then, by assumption 3,

$$\frac{\dot{Y}}{Y} = \frac{1}{Y}\left[\sum_{i=1}^{n} F_i(X_i\dot{A}_i + A_i\dot{X}_i)\right]$$

$$= \frac{1}{Y}\left[\sum_{i=1}^{n} F_i\left(A_iX_i\frac{\dot{A}_i}{A_i} + A_iX_i\frac{\dot{X}_i}{X_i}\right)\right]$$

$$= \sum_{i=1}^{n} F_iA_i\frac{X_i}{Y}\left(\frac{\dot{A}_i}{A_i} + \frac{\dot{X}_i}{X_i}\right)$$

$$= \sum_{i=1}^{n} \frac{\partial F}{\partial X_i}\frac{X_i}{F}\left(\frac{\dot{A}_i}{A_i} + \frac{\dot{X}_i}{X_i}\right)$$

where

$$F_i = \frac{\partial F}{\partial(A_iX_i)}$$

Hence,

$$\frac{\dot{Y}}{Y} = \sum_{i=1}^{n} \alpha_i\left(\frac{\dot{A}_i}{A_i} + \frac{\dot{X}_i}{X_i}\right) \tag{7-2}$$

where $\alpha_i = w_{iX_i}/Y$. Equivalently,

$$\frac{\dot{Z}}{Z} = \alpha\frac{\dot{A}}{A} + \beta\frac{\dot{B}}{B} - \alpha\frac{\dot{X}}{X} \tag{7-3}$$

for the two-factor case $Y = F[A(t)K, B(t)L]$, where $Z = Y/L$ and $X = L/K$.

Define the partial elasticities of substitution with biased technical progress:

$$\sigma_{ij} = \frac{\partial(A_iX_i)/(A_jX_j)}{\partial(F_j/F_i)} \cdot \frac{F_j/F_i}{A_iX_i/A_jX_j}$$

$$= \frac{\dot{A}_i/A_i - \dot{A}_j/A_j + \dot{X}_i/X_i - \dot{X}_\xi/X_j}{\dot{A}_i/A_i - \dot{A}_j/A_j - \dot{w}_i/w_i + \dot{w}_j/w_j} \qquad i, j = 1, \ldots, n$$

By Euler's theorem, and using assumption 3,

$$\frac{\dot{Y}}{Y} = \sum_{i=1}^{n} \frac{\dot{w}_i X_i + \dot{X}_i w_i}{Y} \tag{7–4}$$

Subtracting (7–4) from (7–2) yields

$$\sum_{i=1}^{n} \left(- \frac{X_i \dot{w}_i}{Y} + \alpha_i \frac{\dot{A}_i}{A_i} \right) = 0 \quad \text{or} \quad \sum_{i=1}^{n} \left(- \alpha_i \frac{\dot{w}_i}{w_i} + \alpha_i \frac{\dot{A}_i}{A_i} \right) = 0$$

which is equivalent to the $n - 1$ independent equations:

$$\frac{\dot{w}_i}{w_i} = \frac{\dot{A}_i}{A_i} + \sum_{j \neq i}^{n} \alpha_j \left(\frac{\dot{A}_j}{A_j} - \frac{\dot{A}_i}{A_i} - \frac{\dot{w}_j}{w_j} + \frac{\dot{w}_i}{w_i} \right) \qquad i = 1, \ldots, n - 1$$

using $\Sigma_{k=1}^{n} \alpha_k = 1$. By the definition of σ_{ij}, this reduces to

$$\frac{\dot{w}_i}{w_i} = \frac{\dot{A}_i}{A_i} - \sum_{j \neq i} \frac{\alpha_j}{\sigma_{ij}} \left(\frac{\dot{A}_i}{A_i} - \frac{\dot{A}_j}{A_j} + \frac{\dot{X}_i}{X_i} - \frac{\dot{X}_j}{X_j} \right) \qquad i = 1, \ldots, n - 1 \tag{7–5}$$

The n equations (7–5) and (7–2) are independent and linear in the $\dot{A}_i/A_i$, $\dot{w}_i/w_i$, and $\dot{X}_i/X_i$, and thus equivalent to a system:

$$\frac{\dot{A}_j}{A_j} = \sum_{j=1}^{n} \left[c_{ij} \frac{\dot{X}_j}{X_j} + d_{ij} \frac{\dot{w}_j}{w_j} \right] \qquad i = 1, \ldots, n \tag{7–6}$$

where each coefficient c_{ij} and d_{ij} is a function of the σ_{ij}s and α_js. In the two-factor case, the system of equations (7–3) and (7–5) can be reduced to the two independent equations (Sato, 1970)

$$\frac{\dot{A}}{A} = \frac{\sigma(\dot{\pi}/\pi) - \dot{y}/y}{\sigma - 1} \tag{7–5}$$

$$\frac{\dot{B}}{B} = \frac{\sigma(\dot{w}/w) - \dot{Z}/Z}{\sigma - 1} \tag{7–6}$$

where $y = Y/K$ and $Z = Y/L$.

If we knew the σ_{ij}s, we could use the equations (7–6) to estimate the $\dot{A}_i/A_i$, $i = 1, \ldots, n$. Because each σ_{ij} is itself a parameter to be estimated, without further specification of the nature of σ_{ij}, $i, j = 1, \ldots, n$, the problem remains intractable. (This is the "Impossibility Theorem" of Diamond, McFadden, and Rodriguez, 1978). However, we note that the factor augmenting assumption 3 is consistent with and is in fact implied by a relationship of the form $\sigma_{ij} = \Phi_{ij}(\alpha_i, \alpha_j)$, $i, j = 1, \ldots, n$. Then one of the following assumptions makes the estimation possible:

Assumption 5: $\sigma_{ij} = c_{ij}$, c_{ij} a constant > 0 (or equivalently, the production function is CES).

Assumption 6: $\sigma_{ij} = \gamma_{ij}\alpha_i$ or $\sigma_{ij} = \delta_{ij}\alpha_j$; γ_{ij} and δ_{ij} constants > 0 (or equivalently the production function is CEDD).

Sato (1970) uses the average values of $\dot{A}/A(t)$ and $\dot{B}/B(t)$, computed first under assumption 5 and then under assumption 6, to test the reliability of respectively, the CES and CEDD functions, as long-run models. Woodward (1982) suggests an inverse procedure that can be used to estimate variable rates of biased technical change. He suggests using an assumption of constant rates of technical change (corresponding to average rates), and an assumption of a particular functional form (e.g., assumption 5, assumption 6, or translog), to generate a series of elasticities. The series of elasticities along with equations (7–5) and (7–6) can then be used to estimate the variable rates of technical progress.

7.4. Estimation of the Scale Effect

Now recall Example A and the Kendrick-Sato (1963) method. It follows from Example A that the Kendrick-Sato method is not admissible, because this method assumes a homothetic production function and neutral technical progress. In fact, suppose that, instead of assuming the linear homogeneous production function $f(K, L)$, Kendrick and Sato had allowed for the possibility of increasing returns to scale and had used a production function of the form $N[f(K, L)]f(K, L)$ where N is a Hicks-neutral scale factor. Suppose technical progress were still neutral, factor augmenting. Then the Kendrick-Sato estimation equation would become:

$$\frac{\dot{T}}{T} = \frac{\dot{Y}}{Y} - \frac{\dot{N}}{N} - \left[\alpha\frac{\dot{K}}{K} + \beta\frac{\dot{L}}{L}\right]$$

This is a single equation in the two unknowns $\dot{T}/T$ and $\dot{N}/N$. Because the homothetic family is holothetic under neutral technical progress, the Kendrick-Sato method cannot be extended to permit separate estimation of returns to scale and technical progress.

Next, recall Example B and the Sato (1970) method for the two-factor case. It follows from Example B that this method is admissible, because it assumes a homothetic (*not* almost homothetic) production function and non-neutral technical progress. We should be able to modify it in such a way that it can be used to estimate both technical progress and scale effects. We can modify it in the following manner.

Instead of the linear homogeneous function $f(K, L)$, we allow for the possibility of increasing returns to scale and use a production function of the form $N[f(K, L)]f(K, L)$; suppose that technical progress is still nonuniform. Then the three equations (7–3) and (7–5) become, respectively,

$$\frac{\dot{Z}}{Z} = \alpha\frac{\dot{A}}{A} + \beta\frac{\dot{B}}{B} - \alpha\frac{\dot{X}}{X} + \frac{\dot{N}}{N} \tag{7–3'}$$

and

$$\text{(i)}\quad \frac{\dot{w}}{w} = \frac{\dot{B}}{B} + \frac{\dot{N}}{N} - \frac{\alpha}{\sigma}\frac{\dot{B}}{B} - \frac{\dot{A}}{A} + \frac{\dot{X}}{X}$$

(7–5″)

$$\text{(ii)}\quad \frac{\dot{\pi}}{\pi} = \frac{\dot{A}}{A} + \frac{\dot{N}}{N} + \frac{\beta}{\sigma}\frac{\dot{B}}{B} - \frac{\dot{A}}{A} + \frac{\dot{X}}{X}$$

From (7–3′) we have

$$\text{(I)}\qquad \frac{\dot{N}}{N} = \frac{\dot{Z}}{Z} - \alpha\frac{\dot{A}}{A} - \beta\frac{\dot{B}}{B} + \alpha\frac{\dot{X}}{X}$$

Substituting this into (7–5″-i), we have

$$\frac{\dot{w}}{w} = \frac{\dot{B}}{B} + \left(\frac{\dot{Z}}{Z} - \alpha\frac{\dot{A}}{A} - \beta\frac{\dot{B}}{B} + \alpha\frac{\dot{X}}{X}\right) - \frac{\alpha}{\sigma}\left(\frac{\dot{B}}{B} - \frac{\dot{A}}{A} + \frac{\dot{X}}{X}\right)$$

(7–6)

$$= \alpha\frac{\dot{B}}{B} - \frac{\alpha}{\sigma}\frac{\dot{B}}{B} - \alpha\frac{\dot{A}}{A} + \frac{\alpha}{\sigma}\frac{\dot{A}}{A} + \frac{\dot{Z}}{Z} + \alpha\frac{\dot{X}}{X} - \frac{\alpha}{\sigma}\frac{\dot{X}}{X}$$

This yields

$$\text{(II)}\qquad \frac{\dot{w}}{w} - \frac{\dot{Z}}{Z} - \frac{(\alpha\sigma - \alpha)}{\sigma}\frac{\dot{X}}{X} = \frac{(\alpha\sigma - \alpha)}{\sigma}\frac{\dot{B}}{B} - \frac{(\alpha\sigma - \alpha)}{\sigma}\frac{\dot{A}}{A}$$

Also,

$$\frac{\dot{\pi}}{\pi}=\frac{\dot{A}}{A}+\left(\frac{\dot{Z}}{Z}-\alpha\frac{\dot{A}}{A}-\beta\frac{\dot{B}}{B}+\alpha\frac{\dot{X}}{X}\right)+\frac{\beta}{\sigma}\left(\frac{\dot{B}}{B}-\frac{\dot{A}}{A}+\frac{\dot{X}}{X}\right)$$

$$=\beta\frac{\dot{A}}{A}-\frac{\beta}{\sigma}\frac{\dot{A}}{A}+\frac{\dot{Z}}{Z}-\beta\frac{\dot{B}}{B}+\frac{\beta}{\sigma}\frac{\dot{B}}{B}+\alpha\frac{\dot{X}}{X}+\frac{\beta}{\sigma}\frac{\dot{X}}{X}$$

yields

$$\textbf{(III)}\qquad \frac{\dot{\pi}}{\pi}-\frac{\dot{Z}}{Z}-\frac{(\alpha\sigma+\beta)}{\sigma}\frac{\dot{X}}{X}=-\frac{\beta\alpha+\beta}{\sigma}\frac{\dot{B}}{B}+\frac{\beta\sigma-\beta}{\sigma}\frac{\dot{A}}{A}$$

Let us check the independence of equations II and III. We have:

$$\begin{vmatrix} \dfrac{(\alpha\sigma-\alpha)}{\sigma} & \dfrac{-(\alpha\sigma-\alpha)}{\sigma} \\[2ex] \dfrac{-(\beta\sigma+\beta)}{\sigma} & \dfrac{(\beta\sigma-\beta)}{\sigma} \end{vmatrix}$$

$$=\frac{(\alpha\sigma-\alpha)(\beta\sigma-\beta)}{\sigma^2}-\frac{(\alpha\sigma-\alpha)(\beta\sigma+\beta)}{\sigma^2}$$

$$=\frac{(\alpha\beta\sigma^2-2\alpha\beta\sigma+\alpha\beta)-(\alpha\beta\sigma^2-\alpha\beta)}{\sigma^2}$$

$$=\frac{-2\alpha\beta\sigma+2\alpha\beta}{\sigma^2}=0 \qquad \text{if and only if } \sigma=1$$

Thus, if $\sigma\neq 1$, we can use equations II and III to estimate the rates of technical progress $\dot{A}/A$ and $\dot{B}/B$ and then use equation I to estimate the scale effect. Note that $\sigma=1$ yields a Cobb-Douglas production function, which belongs to the almost homothetic as well as the homothetic class. The Cobb-Douglas is, therefore, holothetic under nonuniform technical progress. This fact can explain why the Cobb-Douglas is the exceptional case and cannot be used for the estimation of nonuniform technical progress and the scale effect.

We can conclude that a technique for estimating technical progress will be admissible so long as the production function is not holothetic under the type of technical progress being estimated.

7.5. The Lie Operator Technique for Estimating Productivity

In the language of Lie group theory, the *infinitesimal operator* corresponding to a Lie transformation group T: $\bar{X}_i = \Phi^i(X_1, \ldots, X_n, \tau)$, $i = 1, \ldots, n$, is the differential operator

$$U = \sum_{i=1}^{n} \xi^i (X) \frac{\partial}{\partial X^i}$$

$$\text{where } X = (X_1, \ldots, X_n) \text{ and } \quad \xi^i (X) = \frac{\partial \Phi^i}{\partial \tau} \Big|_{\tau=0}$$

This should be a familiar expression since $UF = G(f)$ is exactly the partial differential equation for the technology holothetic under T.

If $Y = f(\bar{X}_1, \ldots, \bar{X}_n)$ is a production function, where T: $\bar{X}_i = \Phi^i(X_1, \ldots, X_n, \tau)$, $i = 1, \ldots, n$, is a Lie transformation group, then

$$\frac{\partial}{\partial \tau} [f(X_1, \ldots, X_n, \tau)] \big|_{\tau=0} = Uf = \sum_{i=1}^{n} \xi_i(X) \frac{\partial}{\partial X^i} [f(X_1, \ldots, X_n, 0)] \tag{7–7}$$

Aggregate productivity is generally measured by the Kendrick-Solow productivity index:

$$\frac{\dot{T}}{T} \equiv \frac{\dot{Y}}{Y} - \sum_{i=1}^{n} \frac{X_i}{f(\bar{X}_1, \ldots, \bar{X}_n)} \frac{\partial f}{\partial X_i} \frac{\dot{X}_i}{X_i} \tag{7–8}$$

which is exactly $(\partial f/\partial \tau)/f$. Hence,

$$\sum_{i=1}^{n} \frac{\xi^i(X)}{f} \left(\frac{\partial f}{\partial X_i} \right) \big|_{\tau=0} + \frac{\dot{T}}{T} \big|_{\tau=0} \tag{7–9}$$

Under the following set of conditions these equations can provide a method for estimating the parameters of the functions Φ^i, $i = 1, \ldots, n$.

(i) We assume that $\partial f/\partial X_i = \pi_i =$ the real return to factor i, or that $(\partial f/\partial X_i)\, X_i/Y =$ the relative share of factor i, $i = 1, \ldots, n$.

(ii) We assume that $t = \varepsilon t$, where τ is the parameter of the technical progress or transformation group, t is time, and ε is a constant.

(iii) We define a period to be an interval of time $[t_0, t_1]$ which is small enough that $\dot{T}/T$ as estimated by

$$\frac{\Delta Y}{Y(t_0)} - \sum_{i=1}^{n} \pi_i(t_0)\frac{\Delta X}{X(t_0)}\,\frac{X(t_0)}{Y(t_0)} \qquad (7\text{–}8')$$

where

$$\Delta Y = Y(t_1) - Y(t_0)$$
$$\Delta X = X(t_1) - X(t_0)$$

equation (7–8′) above can be a meaningful approximation to

$$\frac{1}{f}\cdot\frac{\partial f}{\partial \tau}\Big|_{\tau=0}$$

(iv) We assume that the infinitesimal operator of the technical progress transformation is the same in each period $[t_0, t_1]$ and is given by $\Sigma_{i=1}^{n}\ \xi^i(X)\ \partial/\partial X_i$ where $X = X(t_0)$.

Given conditions (i), (ii), (iii), and (iv), if we estimate $\dot{T}/T$ in each period using equation (7–8′) we may be able to apply the regression equation,

$$\frac{\dot{T}}{T} = \sum_{i=1}^{n}\left[\xi_i(X)\cdot\frac{\pi_i}{Y}\right] \qquad (7\text{–}10)$$

to estimate the parameters of the ξ_is.

Note that if we have estimated the parameters of technical progress using the above procedure, then we have circumvented the impossibility theorem of Sato (1970), and of Diamond, McFadden, and Rodriguez (1978). In other words, we have estimated technical progress independently of the form of the production function.

We now present several cases in which this parameter estimation can be accomplished, given conditions (i)–(iv).

Case 1: Suppose that in each period, $Y = f(e^{a\tau}K,\ e^{b\tau}L)$, where f is homogeneous of degree one. Equation (7–10) becomes

$$\frac{\dot{T}}{T} = a\pi\frac{K}{r} + bw\frac{L}{Y}$$

or

$$\frac{\dot{T}}{T} = a + (b - a)\left[w\frac{L}{Y}\right] \qquad (7\text{--}10')$$

$\dot{T}/T$ can be estimated independently using (7–8′). Then (7–10′) is a linear regression equation with $\dot{T}/T$ as the dependent variable and $w(L/Y)$ as the independent variable. The parameters a and $(b - a)$ can be estimated as the coefficients of the regression.

Case 2: Suppose technical progress in each period is the general projective type:

$$T:\quad \bar{K} = \frac{a_1\tau + e^{a_3\tau}K + a_5\tau L}{1 - a_7\tau K - a_8\tau L} \qquad \bar{L} = \frac{a_2\tau + a_4\tau K + e^{a_6\tau}L}{1 - a_7\tau K - a_8\tau L}$$

Then equation (7–10) becomes:

$$\frac{\dot{T}}{T} = \frac{\pi}{Y}(a_1 + a_3K + a_5L + a_7K^2 + a_8KL)$$

$$+ \frac{w}{Y}(a_2 + a_4K + a_6L + a_7KL + a_8L^2)$$

or

$$Y\left(\frac{\dot{T}}{T}\right) = a_1\pi + a_2w + a_3\pi K + a_4wK + a_5\pi L + a_6wL$$

$$+ a_7(K^2\pi + LKw) + a_8(L^2w + KL\pi) \qquad (7\text{--}10'')$$

This is a regression equation that can be used to estimate the parameters $a_1, \ldots, a_8$ as coefficients of the respective variables

$$\pi,\ w,\ \pi K,\ \pi L,\ wL,\ (K^2\pi + KLw) \qquad \text{and} \qquad (L^2w + KL\pi)$$

Note that, in general, if the function $f(\bar{K},\bar{L})$ is to be linear homogeneous, then $a_7 = a_8 = 0$. We may set $a_7 = a_8 = 0$ in equation (7–10″), or we may use equation (7–10″) as is to test the hypothesis $a_7 = a_8 = 0$ and confirm the linear homogeneity of the production function.

Case 3: Suppose $Y = f(\bar{K}, \bar{L})$. We may extend the above technique to cases in which the technical progress transformations $\bar{K} = \Phi(K, L, \tau)$, $\bar{L} = \psi(K, L, \tau)$ do not form a Lie group if the "infinitesimal transformation"

$$U \equiv \frac{\partial \Phi}{\partial \tau}\bigg|_{\tau=0} \frac{\partial}{\partial K} + \frac{\partial \psi}{\partial \tau}\bigg|_{\tau=0}$$

is defined for all K and L in an appropriate domain. If such a U exists, equations (7–7)–(7–9) are satisfied. Thus, if conditions (i)–(iv) hold, we may be able to use equation (7–10) to estimate the parameters of technical progress. For instance, suppose $Y = f(\bar{K}, \bar{L})$ is such that $\partial Y/\partial K = \pi$ and $\partial Y/\partial L = w$ and suppose that in each period

$$\bar{K} = K \exp[(a_1/K + a_3 + a_5 L/K + a_7 K + a_8 L)\tau]$$
$$\bar{L} = L \exp[(a_2/K + a_4 K/L + a_6 + a_7 K + a_8 L)\tau]$$

These do not form a group, but the infinitesimal operator exists for all K and L and is given by

$$U = (a_1 + a_3 K + a_5 L + a_7 K + a_8 KL)\frac{\partial}{\partial K}$$

$$+ (a_2 + a_4 K + a_6 L + a_7 KL + a_8 L)\frac{\partial}{\partial L}$$

Equation (7–10) becomes

$$Y\frac{\dot{T}}{T} = a_1\pi + a_2 w + a_3 \pi K + a_4 w K + a_5 \pi L + a_6 w L$$

$$+ a_7(K^2\pi + LKw) + a_8(L^2 w + KL\pi)$$

which can be used as a regression equation to estimate the a_i, $i = 1, \ldots, 8$.

As an addendum to the above discussion, we note that if the technical progress transformations, $\bar{X}_i = \Phi^i(X, \tau)$, $i = 1, \ldots, n$, are such that an infinitesimal operator

$$U = \sum_{i=1}^{n} \frac{\partial \Phi^i}{\partial \tau}\bigg|_{\tau=0} \frac{\partial}{\partial X_i}$$

is defined for all X in an appropriate domain (in particular, if technical progress is a Lie type), then the following equation will be satisfied by $Y = f(\bar{X}_1, \ldots, \bar{X}_n)$:

$$\sum_{i=1}^{n} \frac{\xi^i(\bar{X}_1, \ldots, \bar{X}_n)}{f(\bar{X}_1, \ldots, \bar{X}_n)} \frac{\partial f}{\partial X_i}(\bar{X}_1, \ldots, \bar{X}_n) = \frac{\dot{T}}{T} \forall \tau \quad (7\text{–}11)$$

where $\xi^i = (\partial \Phi^i/\partial \tau)|_{\tau=0}$

If technical progress is specified to be the factor augmenting type (as in Case 1):

$$T^*:\quad \bar{X}_i = e^{a_i\tau} X_i \qquad \text{or} \qquad \xi^i = a_i X_i$$

then equation (7–11) reduces to

$$\sum_{i=1}^{n} \frac{a_i X_i}{Y} \frac{\partial f}{\partial X_i} = \frac{\dot{T}}{T} \;\forall \tau \tag{7–12}$$

If conditions (i), (ii), and (iii) hold, then equation (7–12) can be used to estimate the parameters a_i. Condition (iv) is not relevant here. We don't need to specify the form of technical progress in each period. Equation (7–12) follows from having defined the long-run technical progress transformation to be the factor augmenting type T^*.

7.6. The Effect of Technical Progress Represented by New Forms of the Production Function

Suppose the technical progress transformation T: $\bar{X}_i = \Phi^i(x_1, \ldots, x_n, \tau)$ is a Lie transformation group. The effect of T on production may be approximated for small τ by the "first order measure" $\tau Uf(K, L, 0)$; i.e., for small τ, $f(K, L, \tau) \cong f(K, L, 0) + \tau Uf(K, L, 0)$. Here U is the infinitesimal operator corresponding to T. If f is not holothetic under T then $Uf(K, L, 0) = g(K, L)$ where $g(K, L) \neq F[f(K, L)]$. This reveals that a new "composite" production function $f(K, L, 0) + \tau g(K, L)$ arises through a technical progress or Lie transformation of the base production function $f(K, L, 0) = f(K, L)$. Given an $f(K, L)$ and a $g(K, L)$ we can find an infinitesimal transformation U corresponding to a Lie group T such that $Uf = g$. (Merely choose $\xi(K, L)$ and $\eta(K, L)$ such that $\xi(\partial f/\partial K) + \eta(\partial f/\partial L) = g(K, L)$, and define $U = \xi(\partial/\partial K) + \eta(\partial/\partial L)$.) In Table 7–1, for exemplary pairs of f and g we define such an infinitesimal operator U which satisfies $Uf = g$.

The technical progress transformation T, whose infinitesimal operator U satisfies $Uf = g$ for a given f and g, may be a useful form of technical progress to assume. For instance, suppose f is homogeneous of degree one; e.g., $f = (aK^{-\rho} + bL^{-\rho})^{-1/\rho}$, and suppose g is log linear; e.g., $g = AK^{\alpha}L^{\beta}$. Suppose that conditions (i)–(iv) of section 7.5 hold, and that technical progress is such that $Uf = g$. We may estimate $\dot{T}/T$ for each period using equation (7–8), and then estimate the parameters of $g(K, L)$ using the equation $\log Y(\dot{T}/T) = \log g(K, L)$. This enables us to characterize technical progress in each period (i.e., for small τ) by the production function $g(K, L)\tau$.

There is another instance in which it is useful to assume that technical progress is of a form such that $Uf = g$. This is the case in which the equation $f(K, L, \tau) \cong f(K, L, 0) + \tau g(K, L) + \pi\Delta K + W\Delta L$ may be used directly to estimate the extent of productivity growth, for τ not too large. For example, suppose f is linear; $f = a_1K + a_2L$, and suppose g is quadratic; $g = b_1K^2 + b_2LK + b_3L^2$. Suppose conditions (i)–(iv) of section 7.5 hold and the following condition (v) holds:

(v) $[t_0, t_1]$ is small enough that

$$f(K, L, \varepsilon t_1) \cong f(K, L, 0) + \varepsilon t_1 g(K, L) + \pi(t_0)\Delta K + w(t_0)\Delta L$$

Let technical progress in each period correspond to the infinitesimal transformation U in block 1 of Table 7–1. Then we have

$$f(K, L, \tau) = a_1K + a_2L + \tau(b_1K^2 + b_2LK + b_3L^2) + \pi\Delta K + W\Delta L$$

We can estimate the parameters a_1, a_2, b_1, b_2, b_3 by the regression equation $Y = f(K, L, \tau)$ and then compute the productivity change in each period, $(b_1K^2 + b_2LK + b_3L^2)\tau$. As another example, let $\log f = a_1 \log K + b_1 \log L$ and let $g = a_2(\log L)^2 + b_2(\log L)^2 + c \log K \log L$. Suppose that conditions (i)–(v) hold and that technical progress in each period corresponds to the infinitesimal transformation U in block 10 of Table 7–1. Then, we have:

$$\log f(K, L, \tau) \cong a_1 \log K + b_1 \log L + \tau(a_2(\log K)^2 + b_2(\log L)^2 + c \log K \log L) + \frac{1}{f(K, L, 0)}(\pi\Delta K + W\Delta L)$$

This is, of course, a well-known translog type production function (Christensen, Jorgenson, and Lau, 1973). The infinitesimal transformation U generated the translog addition. We can estimate the parameters a_1, a_2, b_1, b_2, and c by the regression equation $Y = f(K, L, \tau)$, and then compute the productivity change in each period,

$$\tau(a_2(\log K)^2 + b_2(\log L)^2 + c(\log K)(\log L)$$

Table 7-1

Production Function f	Production: Quadratic: $Y = b_1K^2 + b_2LK + b_3L^2$	CES: $Y = b_1K^{-\delta} + b_2L^{-\delta}$
Linear: $Y = a_1K + a_2L$	1. $\xi = \frac{b_1}{a_1}K^2 - \frac{b_2}{2a_1}KL$ $\eta = \frac{b_3}{a_2}L^2 - \frac{b_2}{2a_2}KL$	2. $\xi = \frac{b_1}{a_1}K^{-\delta}$ $\eta = \frac{b_2}{a_2}L^{-\delta}$
C.D.: $Y = K^{\alpha}L^{\beta}$	6. $\xi = \frac{b_1}{\alpha}K^{3-\alpha}L^{-\beta} + \frac{b_2}{2\alpha}K^{2-\alpha}L^{1-\beta}$ $\eta = \frac{b_3}{\beta}L^{3-\beta}K^{-\alpha} + \frac{b_2}{2\beta}L^{2-\beta}K^{1-\alpha}$	7. $\xi = \frac{b_1}{\alpha}K^{1-\alpha-\delta}$ $\eta = \frac{b_2}{\beta}L^{1-\beta-\delta}$

Function g		
	C. D.	*Translog*
γK	$Y = AK^{\bar{\alpha}} L^{\bar{\beta}}$	$Y = a_2(\log K)^2 + b_2(\log L)^2 + c \log K \log L$
3.	**4.**	**5.**
$\xi = \frac{\gamma}{2a_1} K$	$\xi = \frac{A}{2a_1} K^{\bar{\alpha}} L^{\bar{\beta}}$	$\xi = \frac{a_2}{a_1} (\log K)^2 + \frac{c}{2a_1} \log K \log L$
$\eta = \frac{\gamma}{2a_2} K$	$\eta = \frac{A}{2a_2} K^{\bar{\alpha}} L^{\bar{\beta}}$	$n = \frac{b_2}{b_1} (\log L)^2 + \frac{c}{2a_1} \log K \log L$
8.	**9.**	**10.**
$\xi = \frac{\gamma}{2\alpha} K^{2-\alpha} L^{-\beta}$	$\xi = \frac{A}{2\alpha} K^{\bar{\alpha}-\alpha+1} L^{\bar{\beta}-\beta}$	
$\eta = \frac{\gamma}{2\beta} L^{1-\beta} K^{1-\alpha}$	$\eta - \frac{A}{22\beta} K^{\bar{\alpha}-\alpha} L^{\bar{\beta}-\beta+1}$	

(*Continued next page*)

Table 7–1 *continued*

		Production
Production function of	*Quadratic:*	*CES:*
$\log f = a_1 \log K + b_1 \log L$		
CES:	**11.**	**12.**
$Y = (aK^{-\rho} + bL^{-\rho})^{-1/\rho} = h^{-1/\rho}$	$\xi = \left(\frac{b_1}{a} K^{3+\rho} + \frac{b_2}{2a} K^{2+\rho} L\right) \times h^{1+1/\rho}$	$\xi = \frac{b_1}{a} K^{\rho+1-\delta} h^{1+(1/\rho)}$
where $h \equiv (aK^{-\rho} + bL^{-\rho})$	$\eta = \left(\frac{b_3}{b} L^{3+\rho} + \frac{b_3}{2b} KL^{2+\rho}\right) \times h^{1+1/\rho}$	$\eta = \frac{b_2}{b} L^{\rho+1-\delta} h^{1+(1/\rho)}$

Function g		
	C. D.	Translog
		$\xi = \frac{K}{a_1} a_2(\log K)^2$
		$+ c_2(\log K \log L)$
		$\eta = \frac{L}{b_1} b_2(\log L)^2$
		$+ c_2(\log K \log L)$
13.	14.	
$\xi = \frac{\gamma}{2a} K^{\rho+2} h^{1+(1/\rho)}$	$\xi = \frac{A}{2a} K^{\rho+1+\bar{\alpha}} L^{\bar{\beta}} h^{(1/\rho)+1}$	
$\eta = \frac{\gamma}{2b} KL^{\rho+1} h^{1+(1/\rho)}$	$\eta = \frac{A}{2b} K^{\bar{\alpha}} L^{\rho+1+\bar{\beta}} \times h^{1+1/\rho}$	

References

Berndt, E., and M. Khaled, 1979, "Parametric Productivity Measurement and Choice Among Flexible Functional Forms," *Journal of Political Economy* 87, no. 6:1220–1245.

Binswanger, H. P., 1974, "The Measurement of Technical Change Bias with Many Factors of Production," *American Economic Review* 64:964–976.

Christensen, L., and W. Greene, 1976, "Economies of Scale in U.S. Electric Power Generation," *Journal of Political Economy* 84, no. 4 (pt. 1):655–676.

Christensen, L, R.; D. W. Jorgenson; and L. J. Lau, 1973, "Transcendental Logarithmic Production Frontiers," *Review of Economics and Statistics* 55:28–45.

Denny, M., and J. D. May, 1979, "Factor-Augmenting Technical Progress and Productivity in U.S. Manufacturing," *International Economic Review* 20, no. 3: 759–774.

Diamond, P.; D. McFadden, and M. Rodriguez, 1978, "Measurement of the Elasticity of Factor Substitution and Bias of Technical Change," in D. Fuss and D. McFadden, eds., *Production Economics: A Dual Approach to Theory and Application,* vol. 2, (Amsterdam: North-Holland).

Greene, W. H., 1982, "Simultaneous Estimation of Factor Substitution, Economies of Scale, Productivity, and Non-Neutral Technological Change," chapter 6 of this volume.

Hahn, F. H., and R. C. O. Matthew, 1964, "The Theory of Economic Growth: A Survey," *Economic Journal* vol: 74 851–891.

Kendrick, J. W., and R. Sato, 1963, "Factor Prices, Productivity, and Economic Growth," *American Economic Review* 53:974–1003.

Sato, R., 1970, "The Estimation of Biased Technical Progress and the Production Function," *International Economic Review* 11:179–208.

Sato, R., 1980, "The Impact of Technical Progress on the Holotheticity of Production Functions," *Review of Economic Studies* 47:767–776.

Sato, R., 1981, *The Theory of Technical Change and Economic Invariance: Application of Lie Groups* (New York: Academic Press).

Solow, R. M., 1961, "Comment on Stigler," *Output, Input, and Productivity Measurement, Studies in Income and Wealth,* NBER (Princeton: Princeton University Press.

Stigler, G. J., 1961, "Economic Problems in Measuring Changes in Productivity," *Output, Input, and Productivity Measurement, Studies in Income and Wealth,* NBER (Princeton: Princeton University Press), pp. 47–63.

Woodward, T., 1982, "A Factor Augmenting Approach for Studying Capital Measurement, Obselescence, and the Recent Productivity Slowdown," chapter 5 of this volume.

Name Index

Subject Index